VOLUME 20

JOHN

Norman P. Madsen

ABINGDON PRESS
Nashville

JOHN

Copyright © 1988 by Graded Press

All rights reserved.
No part of this work may be reproduced or transmitted in any form or by any means, electronic or mechanical, including photocopying and recording, or by any information storage or retrieval system, except as may be expressly permitted by the 1976 Copyright Act or in writing from the publisher. Requests for permission should be addressed in writing to Abingdon Press, 201 Eighth Avenue South, Nashville, TN 37203.

This book is printed on recycled, acid-free paper.

ISBN 0-687-02639-3

Library of Congress Cataloging-in-Publication Data

Cokesbury basic Bible commentary.
    Basic Bible commentary/by Linda B. Hinton . . . [et al.].
      p.   cm.
    Originally published: Cokesbury basic Bible commentary. Nashville:
Graded Press © 1988.
    ISBN 0-687-02620-2 (pbk.: v.1: alk. paper)
    1. Bible—Commentaries.   I. Hinton, Linda B.   II. Title.
[BS491.2.C65   1994]
220.7—dc20   94-10965
                                                                                                         CIP

ISBN 0-687-02639-3 (v. 20, John)
ISBN 0-687-02620-2 (v. 1, Genesis)
ISBN 0-687-02621-0 (v. 2, Exodus–Leviticus)
ISBN 0-687-02622-9 (v. 3, Numbers–Deuteronomy)
ISBN 0-687-02623-7 (v. 4, Joshua–Ruth)
ISBN 0-687-02624-5 (v. 5, 1–2 Samuel)
ISBN 0-687-02625-3 (v. 6, 1–2 Kings)
ISBN 0-687-02626-1 (v. 7, 1–2 Chronicles)
ISBN 0-687-02627-X (v. 8, Ezra–Esther)
ISBN 0-687-02628-8 (v. 9, Job)
ISBN 0-687-02629-6 (v. 10, Psalms)
ISBN 0-687-02630-X (v. 11, Proverbs–Song of Solomon)
ISBN 0-687-02631-8 (v. 12, Isaiah)
ISBN 0-687-02632-6 (v. 13, Jeremiah–Lamentations)
ISBN 0-687-02633-4 (v. 14, Ezekiel–Daniel)
ISBN 0-687-02634-2 (v. 15, Hosea–Jonah)
ISBN 0-687-02635-0 (v. 16, Micah–Malachi)
ISBN 0-687-02636-9 (v. 17, Matthew)
ISBN 0-687-02637-7 (v. 18, Mark)
ISBN 0-687-02638-5 (v. 19, Luke)
ISBN 0-687-02640-7 (v. 21, Acts)
ISBN 0-687-02642-3 (v. 22, Romans)
ISBN 0-687-02643-1 (v. 23, 1–2 Corinthians)
ISBN 0-687-02644-X (v. 24, Galatians–Ephesians)
ISBN 0-687-02645-8 (v. 25, Philippians–2 Thessalonians)
ISBN 0-687-02646-6 (v. 26, 1 Timothy–Philemon)
ISBN 0-687-02647-4 (v. 27, Hebrews)
ISBN 0-687-02648-2 (v. 28, James–Jude)
ISBN 0-687-02649-0 (v. 29, Revelation)
ISBN 0-687-02650-4 (complete set of 29 vols.)

Scripture quotations noted NIV are from the HOLY BIBLE, NEW INTERNATIONAL VERSION ®. Copyright © 1973, 1978, 1984 International Bible Society. Used by permission of Zondervan Publishing House. All rights reserved.

Scripture quotations noted NRSV are from the New Revised Standard Version Bible, Copyright © 1989 by the Division of Christian Education of the National Council of the Churches of Christ in the USA. Used by permission.

94 95 96 97 98 99 00 01 02 03—10 9 8 7 6 5 4 3 2 1

MANUFACTURED IN THE UNITED STATES OF AMERICA

Contents

Outline of John

I. The Beginning of the Gospel (1:1-51)
   A. A poetic confession of God's Word (1:1-5)
   B. The sign of John the Baptist (1:6-8)
   C. The Word as the light of the world (1:9-13)
   D. God's Word of grace becomes flesh (1:14-18)
   E. John's witness to the Word (1:19-34)
   F. The first disciples (1:35-51)
II. The Meaning of the Word to Humanity (2:1–4:54)
   A. The new meaning of life (2:1–4:42)
      1. The new wine miracle (2:1-11)
      2. Cleansing of the Temple (2:12-25)
      3. Nicodemus and the new birth (3:1-21)
      4. Testimony of John the Baptist (3:22-36)
      5. The Samaritan woman at the well (4:1-42)
   B. A sign of life's new meaning (4:43-54)
III. Meaning of the Word Within Judaism (5:1–10:42)
   A. Jesus and a Jewish festival (5:1-47)
      1. Healing on the sabbath (5:1-18)
      2. Teachings about healing (5:19-47)
   B. Jesus and a new Passover (6:1-71)
      1. Feeding the five thousand (6:1-15)
      2. Jesus walks on the sea (6:16-21)
      3. Jesus the bread of life (6:22-71)
   C. Jesus and the Feast of Tabernacles (7:1–9:41)
      1. The feast of Tabernacles (7:1-52)
      2. The woman caught in adultery (7:53–8:11)
      3. Jesus the light of the world (8:12-59)

Introduction to John

The early church symbol for the Gospel of John is the eagle. According to the church scholar Jerome (A.D. 349–420), each New Testament Gospel can be identified with one of the four creatures in the vision of Ezekiel (see Ezekiel 1 and 10). One of the four, the eagle, was thought to best represent the Gospel of John. An eagle soars in the heights with majestic patterns of flight. So John's Gospel soars to heaven and swoops back to earth, telling the story of Jesus the Christ. What is known about this majestic Gospel?

The Uniqueness of John's Gospel

John is the odd one out of the four New Testament Gospels. The first three gospels are very similar in content. In fact, they are so similar that Matthew, Mark, and Luke must have somehow used each other as they wrote their versions of the good news. But the Gospel of John is very different from these other Gospels. For example, in John's Gospel Jesus offers no parables; he does not give a long sermon (Sermon on the Mount: Matthew 5–7; Luke 6:17-49); he does not give brief sayings and teachings (Mark 2:27; 3:28-29); he does not heal lepers; all miracles are signs of his identity (and not simply acts of mercy).

John is also unique in its use of opposites or contrasts. The Gospel constantly contrasts light and darkness; miracles and debates with the Jews; Jesus and the disciples with Judaism; and so forth. Embedded in these contrasts is a strong use of symbolism. The Gospel's use of symbolism is not meant to suggest that things did not really happen as presented. Rather, the use of symbolism is an attempt to help the reader penetrate deeper into the greater significance and meaning of events (see the commentary on 6:16-21, for example).

How can the uniqueness of John's Gospel be explained? People, geography, times, and intended purpose influence the writing of any document. These influences are important for understanding the uniqueness of John's Gospel.

The People Behind John's Gospel

The earliest reference to the writer of this Gospel is from the church leader Irenaeus (A.D. 140–203). He states that this Gospel was written in Ephesus by John, the disciple of Jesus. Irenaeus received this information from his teacher, Polycarp (A.D. 70–160), who knew John the apostle personally. But this information must be accepted with some caution, because early church writers have not always been proven correct. Irenaeus was almost certainly referring to John, the son of Zebedee, one of the twelve apostles. Perhaps this John left his masked signature in the Gospel narrative. The Gospel contains several references to a mysterious *beloved disciple* who seems to be present at important points in the story but is never named (see 13:23-25; 18:15-16; 20:2-10, for example).

However, things are not that simple. A good analysis of the text indicates different styles of writing and word choice. This implies editing and revision by different individuals. Hence we will probably never know beyond a doubt the true author or authors of John's Gospel. But we are justified in assuming that John the apostle was somehow behind this Gospel (see 21:24). Perhaps John the apostle wrote the first draft and his followers edited "his" Gospel (see below) after he died, adding stories and accounts that John had personally told them. In the

8

thinking of the first century, if the apostle John was somehow behind the Gospel, it would be said that John wrote the Gospel.

The Location and Date of John's Gospel

The writing of John's Gospel went through various stages. There are three probable levels of development. The first stage began in Palestine. After Jesus' death, John and the other disciples became leaders among those who believed Jesus was the Christ. We do know that John did not immediately leave Palestine (Acts 8:14; Galatians 2:9). During this time in and around Jerusalem, John probably established his own little group of "disciples" or followers. This would have been quite normal. These followers would have been people who not only believed in Jesus, but wanted to learn more about Jesus and his teachings.

The second stage was a major move—for unknown reasons—of John to Ephesus. It is very probable that at least some disciples went with him. Ephesus was a major seaport city in western Asia Minor with a large population. Trade was the main industry in Ephesus. It was also the home of a pagan Greek religion devoted to the mother goddess Artemis (Acts 19:32-34). In this city, an early draft of John's Gospel was probably written. The date of John's arrival in Ephesus and the draft of the Gospel would be after Paul's missionary activity in the city during the 50s. A good estimate for the arrival of John and some of his disciples in Ephesus would be the decade of the 60s.

The third stage is the final writing of John's Gospel. This probably occurred after the death of John. His disciples and followers edited, wrote, and published a final version of the Gospel, holding true to what John had written and taught. The early church understood this Gospel to be John's *testimony* (21:24) to Jesus Christ. The final edition that we find in our New Testament was probably completed between A.D. 80 and 100.

This brings up an intriguing question. Were John and his disciples aware of the other Gospels during these stages of development? Certainly as an eyewitness and an apostle, John would have drawn from the same basic pool of information that influenced the other Gospel writers. But it is more likely that John and his disciples never knew the other Gospels in their finished state as we know them today. If they did know the other Gospels, it was probably in some form of a rough draft.

The Structure of John's Gospel

John is a carefully finished account of Jesus' life. Material was chosen and organized with care to announce a central theme: Eternal life comes through Jesus Christ and this is God's purpose for humanity. This is accomplished in two ways: First, Jesus is directly related to four major Jewish festivals. Second, signs play a very important role, pointing to the central message. For example, there are signs of turning water into wine (2:1-11), healing the sick (4:43-54), feeding the five thousand (6:1-15), and raising Lazarus from the dead (11:1-44). All of these signs point to eternal life through Christ. At the end of the Gospel, the reader is assured that Jesus did additional signs, which the disciples witnessed (20:30). The Gospel also has an introductory chapter, which attempts to prepare the minds of the readers, and a concluding chapter that challenges believers and disciples to follow Jesus (21:22). The structure of John's Gospel is so carefully arranged that it almost certainly reflects the thinking—if not the hand—of John himself.

The Purpose of John's Gospel

This is by far the most important aspect of the Gospel. What was the intention of those behind this writing?

What was the deeper purpose of John the apostle? It seems quite clear that the Gospel is meant to help the reader understand the identity of Jesus as the Messiah and the Son of God and to initiate response to him (see 20:31). But what else can we know about the purpose of John's Gospel?

As noted above, this Gospel is written for early church believers. On the one hand, tradition tells us that John the apostle was involved with a particular congregation or church in Ephesus. Perhaps he was associated with several congregations in and outside of this city. But more than likely one community was his home congregation. This particular congregation was the setting for the formation of John's Gospel. Like all other New Testament documents, John was written with a particular living church situation in mind. On the other hand, through this one congregation, the Gospel addresses all humanity and the church universal. This is the complete audience to whom the message is directed. But with the help of this particular congregation, we can better hear what John is saying about Jesus the Christ.

The social structures of the first century make some useful suggestions about church congregations. Beyond the Gentile/Jewish distinction, an Asia Minor church would have been comprised of two groups of believers: *Jewish* Christians and *Hellenistic* or Greek-influenced Christians. The Jewish believers would tend to see Christ through the Jewish Torah, or law. The Hellenistic Christians would tend to see Christ through Greek philosophy, culture, and wisdom. It would follow that Jewish converts would have difficulty accepting Jesus as more than a man (that is, divine). The Hellenistic Christians would have difficulty thinking of Jesus as less than divine (that is, human) because of the influence of Greek philosophy.

In the middle of these social groups, John's purpose emerged. He seeks to present a very balanced Christ who is more than human as *fully God*, and yet not less than God, having become *fully human*. Christ is the true *mediator* of God and humankind. John then goes on to use Jesus' teachings about love and unity to encourage the congregation(s) to seek oneness in Christ (chapters 13–17). This is John's deeper theological purpose.

John and Related New Testament Writings

The apostle behind the Gospel also influenced the three letters of John and the book of Revelation. The tension noted above between Jewish Christians and Greek or Gentile Christians is probably behind the issues evident in these later writings. The first letter, for example, refers to an *antichrist* withdrawing from the community (1 John 2:18). The second letter speaks of *deceivers* who have *gone out into the world,* but who will not acknowledge *Jesus Christ as come in the flesh;* such a one *is the deceiver and the antichrist* (2 John 7). In the third letter, Diotrephes the troublemaker is referred to as one who *likes to put himself first* (NRSV; NIV, *loves to be first*) and one who *does not acknowledge our authority* (3 John 9 NRSV; NIV, *will have nothing to do with us*). The letters of John and the book of Revelation indicate serious problems among John's followers. They confirm a continued need for a well-balanced, well-organized, and carefully presented witness to Jesus the Christ.

A Final Word

So is the uniqueness of John's Gospel. Knowing a little about the people behind this writing, its city of emergence, its plan and purpose, should help us soar on its wings to the heights of heaven and swoop back to earth for a better understanding of Jesus the Christ.

John 1:1-18

Introduction to These Verses

John's opening chapter contains some of the most profound Christian literature ever produced. Unlike the other Gospels, John begins with eternal things. The intention is not to first establish that Jesus was very human. This Gospel has no interest in family trees or Jewish lineage. The real importance of Jesus the Nazarene lies in his "pre-existence." The starting point of this Gospel is that Jesus existed or lived before the world was created.

The opening verses have been greatly respected throughout history. They have been discovered in lockets or amulets; they have been used to bless the dying, the sick, and the needy; they have been used as a prayer, as part of worship, and as words of reassurance. These opening lines have carried an almost magical quality. They immediately direct the reader to heavenly things.

In order to speak of these heavenly things, the Gospel begins "poetically." Because of our inability to speak of truths that are literally out of this world, poetic verse is helpful. As a result, some have argued that this Gospel begins with a hymn. Certainly these verses could well have been an early hymn to the praise of God's salvation plan for humanity. Perhaps these lines were composed by John and inspired through a vision. And perhaps these verses were sung by churches in and around Ephesus.

The prologue may be divided into four parts.

I. A Poetic Confession of God's Word (1:1-5)
II. The Sign of John the Baptist (1:6-8)
III. The Word as the Light of the World (1:9-13)
IV. God's Word of Grace Becomes Flesh (1:14-18)

A Poetic Confession of God's Word (1:1-5)

The Gospel begins with the same three words as the Old Testament. The start of Genesis reads, *In the beginning . . . God created the heavens and the earth* (Genesis 1:1). The Gospel of John begins, *In the beginning was the Word, and the Word was with God, and the Word was God* (1:1). The analogy is deliberate and meaningful. John is saying poetically, the *Word* is *God* and *God* is the *Word.* The Word of God and God the Word were there in the beginning. They always were and they always will be.

What is the meaning of *Word?* The Greek term *logos* carries the meaning of *personal action.* What a significant term for speaking about Jesus the Christ. He not only is the personal expression of God to humanity, but this word is an action, an act. In the beginning, God "acted personally" toward humanity—toward us. God did not simply speak. God acted. God's speech and God's action are synonymous. For God—and based on God's Word—to speak and act toward us is to get personal and to draw near.

The writer then refers to the *Word* as *He* (verse 2). *He was in the beginning with God.* Exactly how the action of God gets personal and draws near to humanity is a mystery. This Gospel makes it clear from the start that the Word is divine. Jesus the Word is God. The Word will never be less than God. The Word is God. It is amazing—but this Word draws near to humanity as flesh (see verse 14).

Then we read that all things were made through him (verse 3). This statement has traditionally been understood as *Creation.* In this sense, the reader is again brought back to the Genesis Creation accounts. Not only was the Word present when all things were created, but they were created *through, with,* and *for Him.* He is the basis of everything that exists.

It follows that the Word is the purpose of all things. If all things are made or have their being through him, then all things are true, right, and real only in him. He is the reason behind all that is; he is the goal of all things; he is the center of the universe; he is the key to what philosophy calls *reality.* The universe only makes sense in him. He is the beginning and the end. To say the same thing in a negative manner, without him the creation—and humanity, the peak of creation (see Psalm 8)—would be nothing but chaos, the void, the formless space (Genesis 1:2).

This focus on Jesus the Word continues. Because the word is *life,* everything has life in him (verse 4). He alone is life-giving. As life, he is light (see verse 9). Without any light, there would be chaos and darkness. The reassuring truth about the *Word of God* is that chaos and darkness could not extinguish this light (verse 5). In this way the centrality of the Word for the entire universe is affirmed. And this points us back to the first verse.

The Sign of John the Baptist (1:6-8)

After this awesome beginning, the Gospel refers to a supporting event. Looking back to the Old Testament, God promised through the prophets to tell the people when to expect more complete divine words and actions. The prophet Malachi, writing about 400 B.C., tells about a messenger or angel who would *prepare the way* before the Lord, the same Lord whom you seek. He adds, *The messenger of the covenant in whom you delight* (NRSV; NIV, *whom you desire)* is coming, *says the LORD* (Malachi 3:1; see also Isaiah 40:3).

In all four Gospels, this expected messenger is identified as John the Baptist. His task is to indicate

God's new action. God keeps the promises, and sends a messenger to point out God's drawing near. This messenger is one who is equipped to hear and see God's personal action in Christ. In this manner, John represents all humanity who are also equipped, or given the gift of faith. But John is a further example to humanity in that he accepts the gift of faith (the *power*, [NRSV; NIV, *right*], verse 12) and becomes as a child—a child of God. John accepts God's personal action in Christ and accepts his calling to point to and bear witness to the Word.

The Word as the Light of the World (1:9-13)

Now Christ the Word is explained by the analogy of *light* (verse 9). Christ the light does two things. First of all, the true light proclaims the truth of God. The basic truth of the Creation, humanity, the universe, and so forth are all dependent upon the one light of God. Therefore, Christ is the only true light of God that shines in our darkness. At the end of the Gospel, Pilate asks Jesus, *What is truth?* (see John 18:38). But the reader is told at the beginning what is truth—the Word is truth, the true light.

Second, this light enlightens every person. The emphasis is still on the Word. Humanity remains secondary. The Word enlightens because the Word is the key to the universe. The light could do nothing else! As a result, we are enlightened by him. We can know nothing without the enlightening truth. The emphasis remains on the *true light*. Without him, everything is out of focus—we must have the light.

This *light* was already here and was not recognized (verse 10). This is a continuing problem with humanity—the world did not recognize him. Here we are, made *through him* and *for him*, and yet we do not know him. How can this be? Something has gone wrong. Rebellion is evident everywhere; we have turned away from the key to all things. Humans created for God have refused to be children of God—we have sought our own will and have run away.

The next verse pushes this theme of rebellion further (verse 11). The rebellion of the creation is very personal. He came to his own, and he was not received. Following the Genesis themes in the Creation accounts, humanity is created for covenant fellowship with God. In this manner, we are created in the image of God. But humanity rebelled, returning the creation to chaos and darkness (much like the symbolism of Adam and Eve being thrown out of the garden). So now when the one through whom all things were created comes home—his own people received him not.

But the Word is the light of all humanity (verses 12-13). Those who accept this truth become *children of God*. Notice that these persons are given *power*, divine power to become children. Why would God give us the power to become children? (This statement anticipates Jesus' conversation with Nicodemus, in John 2:23–3:21.) The *power* is the gift of faith. Accepting this gift is the beginning of life as a child of God. Thus faith as a child begins with God and comes from God.

A person who accepts the gift of faith no longer acts and thinks from self—or from the side of humanity. The child of God thinks and acts out of God. All the characteristics of a child are meant to be evident in the person who believes. The child of God will trust the Father, accept and obey the will of the Father, experience the greatest joy in being with the Father, and so forth. The child of God seeks the light and runs from the darkness to the safety of the Father. And all this is done by the Father.

This is why John's Gospel begins with heavenly things. Humans are simply asked to become children through Christ, their brother, and to trust the Father. Hence, humanity is *born of God* (verse 13). In this sense, we are not born of *blood* (woman), of *flesh* (lust), or of *man*

(Matthew 16:17; 1 Corinthians 15:50). We are made for God; we are born for God.

God's Word of Grace Becomes Flesh (1:14-18)

These are the last verses of the introduction to the prologue or opening chapter. They function as a summary of what has already been said.

The famous opening verse states the Gospel in miniature (verse 14). This may be the most profound thought and verse in the Christian Bible. It states in a few words what has already been poetically stated and will soon be more fully presented. The *Word* that was with God in the beginning and for whom all is created *become flesh*. In part, this profound thought is incomprehensible—we cannot comprehend God! But with the help of the prayerful poetic beginning, perhaps we can apprehend a portion of God's truth.

The word *flesh* refers to humanity in general. The Word became man, a man, a human being. Out of all the species of creation, the Word became humanity. God freely chose humanity for fellowship with the divine. What a humbling thought! God, in divine freedom, chose to covenant and embrace humanity, speaking on our terms in the flesh so that we could apprehend and hear God's truth.

Dwelling *among us* carries the Old Testament meaning of *tenting* among us. In Exodus 25:8-9, Israel is instructed by God to make a tent (from the Hebrew word meaning *tabernacle)* so God can dwell among or in the midst of the people. In this sense, God dwells, like the people, in a tent. The Israelites at this time were a nomadic people and home was a tent. In such a tent, God chose to be present with Israel (Joel 2:27; Zechariah 2:10; Ezekiel 43:7). Early Jewish thought also stressed the "shekinah promise," or God's promise to always dwell with the people. In this sense, John records how the Word became flesh and lived among us, fulfilling God's continued promise to humanity through Israel. And now this is accomplished once and forever.

Because of God's coming to humanity, God's glory is made known. God willingness to come out of love for the rebellious—the true light in our darkness—is *full of grace and truth*. When the eyewitnesses beheld the Word in the flesh, when the apostles went to the tabernacle or tent (the Christ), they *saw his glory*, the glory of the *only* Son *from the Father*. This event of incarnation (literally, *in the flesh*) is affirmed in the other three Gospels by the event of the Transfiguration (Matthew 17:1-8; Mark 9:2-8; Luke 9:28-36; see also 2 Peter 1:16-17).

Literally in a parenthesis, the witness of John the Baptist is briefly reintroduced (verse 15). The glorious miracle is that John only knew this truth because it was given to him by God (1:33). His message is clear and straightforward (3:22-36): Jesus is the one who *comes after me*. He is the glorious "tabernacled" presence. Because of this truth, John's witness can never displace the Word, the light, the Christ. This danger of displacement remains a current one. Too often the witness or formulation of the truth replaces or eclipses the truth. But only by the full presence of the true Word will all receive *grace upon grace* (verse 16).

The last two verses of the introduction to the prologue state the two occasions when God has drawn close to humanity. This happened first through Moses' establishing the old covenant with the law. After God liberated Israel from Egypt, the law became the guidelines for Israel's covenant response to God. This response was channeled through the old tabernacle experience. But the second, more profound way God drew close to humanity was in the tabernacle of Christ, establishing a new covenant in grace. Now humanity can respond to God in the name of Christ through the permanent tabernacle of the true Word (Hebrews 7:23-25)

How do we really know God? There is an Old

Testament theme that flesh cannot see God and live. Moses desired to see God's glory or see God (Exodus 33:18). He was told that this could not happen if his life were to continue (also see Isaiah 6:5). John's Gospel reflects this Jewish understanding. *No one has ever seen God* (verse 18). But the Son, the Word, the light, the one who tabernacles with us, makes God known. This is an important theme when Jesus gives some last instructions to the disciples (chapter 14). The Son is in the bosom of the Father, in that he is in an eternal and real relationship with the Father. Jesus is beside the Father (see 3:13 and 8:16). From the beginning of Creation to the end of redemption, Christ is the will of the Father.

§ § § § § § §

The Message of John 1:1-18

These verses attempt to prepare readers for what is to come. The gospel or good news is that God has come to humanity. God has not left us alone in the darkness, but has come to tabernacle with us and rescue us from death and destruction. Here are some truths that stretch our minds at the beginning of this Gospel.

§ God acts personally for humanity.
§ God sends the Word—spoken and acted.
§ All creation has its purpose and existence in God's Word.
§ Christ is the light of humanity.
§ Christ is the only place (the tabernacle) where God is found.
§ John the Baptist is a sign of God's true Word.
§ God sends humanity the gift of faith through the Holy Spirit.

§ § § § § § §

John 1:19-51

Introduction to These Verses

The remaining verses of chapter 1 are written in narrative style, a more earthly telling of events. After stretching the reader's mind with poetic wonder and truth, the Gospel turns to the actual story of Jesus' life.

This section has two parts.

I. John's Witness to the Word (1:19-34)

II. The First Disciples (1:35-51)

John's Witness to the Word (1:19-34)

Following the preliminary announcements in verses 1-18, John turns to the message and importance of John the Baptist. This is a rather interesting presentation of the Baptist. John's testimony is presented on three consecutive days, reminding us of the three consecutive days Jesus spends in the tomb, the three post-Resurrectional appearances Jesus makes at the end of the Gospel (21:14), and the three directives Jesus gives to Peter for feeding his sheep (21:15-16). In the first two testimonies, John is asked to define his relation to the one who is to come (verses 19-28), and he does so by telling of Jesus' identity (verses 29-34). The third testimony influences two of John's disciples to follow Jesus, and they become Jesus' first disciples (verse 35). So, John the Baptist's three testimonies are presented in a manner that relates them to the important final events of the Gospel.

John the Baptist is first approached by Jewish

authorities (verses 19-23). They are identified as *Levites* from Jerusalem. These authorities seek John's identity (verse 19). John responds by confessing that he is *not the Christ* (verse 20 NIV; NRSV, *Messiah*). *Confessed* (used twice for emphasis) is clearly meant to carry strong theological overtones. John's task is to *confess*, to point, to direct attention to the messiah. But in case anyone gets confused, John's confession emphasizes that he is not the one. At this time in the first century, there were Jewish groups and movements that were very watchful for the coming one, the messiah. Some of these groups would have been the Essenes (Qumran community), some were Pharisees, and some were Levites. Their question to John is direct: Are you the messiah?

There apparently is some confusion over John's identity and his relation to Jesus. Not only does Jesus gain his first disciples from the followers of John (1:35-51), but later John is still baptizing when a discussion between his disciples and a Jew develops over Jesus' identity (3:22-30). Some did suspect that John the Baptist was the Christ (Luke 3:15); hence the emphasis on confession.

Then John is asked if he is Elijah or a prophet (verses 21-22). An Old Testament tradition said that Elijah would return, marking the new time of the Lord (2 Kings 2:11). And here we find John the Baptist, dressing like Elijah (2 Kings 1:8; Mark 1:6) and coming out of the wilderness just like Elijah (1 Kings 17:1-5; Malachi 4:5). Another tradition was that a prophet similar to Moses would appear (Deuteronomy 18:15-18). So it is not surprising that the Levites question John about his identity.

The Baptist's response is to claim only a preparatory role. Quoting Isaiah 40:3, John states a Jewish hope from the past. During the Babylonian Captivity (about 587–540 B.C.), Isaiah the prophet spoke of God's eventual blessing of a straight road through the desert from Babylon back to the homeland, back to Jerusalem and Palestine. But

John interprets a far greater blessing. God will actually come to the people right away, on a direct road prepared by a messenger. Hence, even though John denies the suggestion that he is Elijah or a prophet, he functions as an Elijah or prophet. His role is to signal the way or manner of the Lord's arrival.

Then John is questioned further (verses 24-28): If you are not the one, then why are you acting in this manner (baptizing) and speaking such a message? Why are you acting with signs that indicate something special or divine is about to happen? John's answer is that his baptism only prepares the way for the one who is to come. John is not even worthy to act as a slave and care for his sandals (verse 27). Further, these very people who are asking John questions and demanding answers will not even recognize *the one* when he comes (verse 26). For all their enthusiasm, they will not come to know the truth. John himself could only recognize the messiah by the power of God.

The last part of this section tells of John the Baptist's second testimony to Jesus (verses 29-34). This direct witness occurs on the second day, apparently after Jesus' baptism. The first part of John's statement (verses 29-31) is the result of seeing Jesus coming toward him. In three verses we find three clear themes of testimony.

First of all, Jesus is identified as the *Lamb of God who takes away the sin of the world* (verse 29). This is a very meaningful phrase in Jewish tradition in the context of the Temple as the center of Jewish worship. The early Christians treated this statement as a reference to the suffering servant found in Isaiah (42:1-4; 49:1-6; 50:4-9; 52:13-15). The suffering servant was one who would fulfill God's plan of salvation for humanity, suffering as a sacrificial lamb of God. (However, it was still unclear if the servant was all of Israel or an individual.) At minimum, John's statement is a reference to the lamb used for Temple sacrifice. The Temple lamb was understood as a sacrifice provided by God for the people.

Second, John moves to a deeper theme (verse 30). He makes reference to Jesus' pre-existence with the Father before Creation. Although Jesus comes after John, he was before him (1:1-5). Because the one who is coming is of God, John's role is to simply lead the way (verse 31). John could not have known this *one* by his own powers of recognition. He confesses this (v. 33). This is a critically important theme. Our recognition of God's coming to us and our hearing God speak to us is only possible through the power (the Holy Spirit) of God. This avoids the issue of whether believers have any part in coming to faith. Surely they do! Based on John the Baptist's recognition of Jesus, it is clear that the believer's role in faith is to accept the truth God makes known on God's terms. Humanity does not reveal God. Only God reveals God. This important truth is then stated again (verse 33), showing its significance for the early church's understanding of John the Baptist's role and relation to Jesus.

Third, John tells about Jesus' baptism. John sees the dove descending on Jesus (verse 32). The dove symbolizes the Holy Spirit coming upon Jesus, equipping him for the work he is about to do. John's Gospel is not so much concerned to tell the readers about the actual baptism of Jesus (as the other Gospels tend to emphasize); John is more concerned to tell of the coming of the Holy Spirit upon Jesus. (This is a theme of the Gospel; see chapters 14–16.) This is the same Spirit that gave John the "eyes" to recognize Jesus. The Spirit remains with Jesus throughout his work of reconciliation between God and humanity (verse 33). Because of God's revelation to John the Baptist (identifying Jesus), and because the Spirit comes fully upon Jesus and remains on him, the Baptist refers to Jesus as the *Son of God* or the messiah. The Spirit of God is eventually released upon humanity because of Christ's work (14:16-17).

The First Disciples (1:35-51)

This general section has two subsections. The first of these smaller sections deals with *two disciples* and Simon Peter meeting Jesus. The second smaller section tells of Philip and Nathanael becomes disciples.

In the first of these sections, we are told it is still the second day (verse 35). John the Baptist is doing what he is called to do—witnessing to Jesus the Messiah. As he stands with two of his disciples, and following his testimony, he unknowingly points two of his disciples to Jesus. John does not point to himself—even in the midst of his own followers. He takes no credit. He wants no attention. He moves to the background and points to Jesus.

Hearing John's testimony (verse 37), the two disciples immediately *followed Jesus. Following* is the theme of these verses (it is also the theme of this Gospel's last chapter). Notice the development of events: The Baptist is able to identify who Christ is by the power of God; by his testimony two of his followers become followers of Jesus the Christ. God not only comes to tabernacle or tent with us, but also gives humanity the eyes to see and ears to hear the message of love for all humanity.

Jesus abruptly asks the two following him what they want (verse 38). They refer to him as *Rabbi,* indicating Jesus was already known as a teacher. They ask him where he stays, attempting to shield their interest to learn more about him and know him better. He responds, *Come* and *see.* Jesus invites them to learn more about himself. Their question is followed by his gentle command.

They do two things in getting to know Jesus: They *fellowship* and they *abide.* One of them is identified as Andrew, the brother of Simon Peter (verse 40). It appears as though Peter is better known to the readers than his brother. Like the Baptist, Andrew now testifies to his brother and introduces his brother to Jesus (verses 41-42). In a very short time, Andrew calls Jesus the *Messiah*, the Christ, the anointed—as a result of their abiding fellowship. In the other Gospels, it took much longer for the apostles to identify Jesus as the Messiah (see Mark 8, for example). Because the disciples eventually abandoned Jesus at Gethsemane, we can assume that they probably only understood the term in retrospect.

Hence early in this Gospel, the *messiah* is connected with Peter. This connection is made here through Peter's name. We are told that by simply looking at Peter, Jesus knew his character. So Peter is given a new name. His new name, *Cephas*, or *Peter*, means *rock* in Aramaic and Greek. Among many ancient societies, a change of name signified a role change within the society (Genesis 17:5; 32:28). Peter's new name refers to the future role he will play as a follower of the messiah. Peter the rock will become the future earthly leader of Jesus' followers, replacing Jesus the rock who will go to the Father.

In the second section the theme of *follow me* is continued. It is the *next day* (verse 43). Jesus wishes to go to Galilee. He finds Philip either before he goes or upon his arrival. Philip, associated with Andrew and Peter, seeks out Nathanael and testifies that Jesus fulfills the entire Old Testament. It is not surprising that Nathanael is sceptical about such a statement. But like the first two disciples, Nathanael is encouraged to *come and see* (verse 46).

In the context of Jewish fulfillment, Nathanael is willing to come to the light of Jesus the Messiah. For this reason, Jesus says there is no *deceit* (NRSV; NIV, *nothing false*; i.e., no craftiness or treachery) in Nathanael (verse 47). He is representative of one who does not hide from God (Genesis 3:8-9) and therefore is an Israelite true to

God (unlike *Jacob,* Genesis 27:35, who is called *Israel,* Genesis 32:28-30).

When Nathanael asks how Jesus knew him, he is told how he was seen under the fig tree. It is interesting that the fig tree is mentioned in Genesis 3:7 as a covering of Adam's and Eve's "sinful" nakedness. Also, Jesus curses a fig tree (Mark 11:12-14; compare Matthew 21:18-19 and Luke 13:6-9). The symbolic meaning of Jesus' curse has to do with the unbelieving Jewish community which chooses sinfulness rather than belief. Unbelieving Israel fails to recognize the true messiah because of human expectations. Further, the fig tree also represents the redeemed life of faithful Israel in the messianic age of peace (see Micah 4:4 and Zechariah 3:10). Thus Nathanael is literally blessed by Jesus for believing, and is called—as all are called—to the new life given in Christ.

Nathanael responds by calling Jesus the *Son of God* and *King of Israel* (verse 49). In the context of *follow me* and *come and see,* Nathanael senses great things in Jesus. The seed of faith is planted (Matthew 13:31-32). The light has flickered on in the "sinful" heart of Nathanael and the darkness has not overcome it. There is no guile here. And Jesus goes on to say *greater things* are going to happen. In other words, the seed of faith in his heart will grow into a marvelous truth so that other hearts will be lighted.

The last verse in this chapter seems to be from another setting. It does fit here, suggesting that the author or editor (redactor) used it to explain the previous verse. This vision statement is probably based upon Jacob's dream in Genesis 28:12. In this present context, Jesus is the *ladder,* the connector, the one who binds heaven and earth together. The *angels* are God's messengers or God's blessings that go back and forth between God and humanity. In this sense, angels are forerunners of the Holy Spirit who is sent in all fullness after Christ's work of reconciliation is complete (14:16-17, 25-26; 15:26-27). In this last section, both *Son of God* (verse 49) and *Son of man* (verse 51) are used to speak of Jesus. He is the Messiah who comes down from heaven as the *Son of God,* fully divine. He is also the *Son of man,* being fully human. As fully God and fully man, Jesus the *mediator* gives new definition and understanding to the term *messiah.*

§ § § § § § §

The Message of John 1:19-51

These verses are narrative in style, rather than poetic. They give a factual account of the work of John the Baptist, and of the calling of Jesus' first disciples. What can we learn from these verses?

§ God calls all persons to discipleship.
§ Discipleship means abiding in fellowship with others.
§ There was a close relationship between John the Baptist and Jesus, as well as among the disciples of each.
§ The ministry of Jesus is closely related to tradition and to history.
§ The Holy Spirit helps us recognize God.
§ God gives us the power to recognize God's promise.

§ § § § § § §

John 2

Introduction to This Chapter

The first real sign Jesus acts out is at the wedding celebration in Cana of Galilee. This unique sign of changing the water into wine is not found elsewhere in the New Testament. This miracle signifies a new day, a new celebration, a new life established through a new covenant between God and humanity. This new covenant relationship will be worked out between the bridegroom, Jesus (3:29), and his bride, the church. The popular Old Testament metaphor of the marriage relationship as representative of God's covenant with Israel is now redefined, turned around, and reestablished.

The theme of the new covenant and new life is affirmed in the sections that follow.

Chapter 2 has two parts.

  I. The New Wine Miracle (2:1-11)

 II. Cleansing of the Temple (2:12-25)

The New Wine Miracle (2:1-11)

This is the first of seven signs John's Gospel records about Jesus. The other six signs all have close—if not exact—parallels in the other Gospels. Three signs are actually found in the synoptic Gospels: the healing of the royal official's son (4:46-54), the feeding of the great crowd (6:1-15), and walking on the sea (6:16-21). Three other signs are similar to accounts found in the other Gospels: the healing of a paralyzed man (5:1-15), healing of a blind man (chapter 9), and raising a dead person (chapter 11). But this particular sign of changing the water into wine stands alone, unique to this Gospel.

The story begins by telling us that it is the *third day.* The third days relates this event to Jesus' resurrection on the third day when he overcame death. So his action at the wedding in Cana of Galilee anticipates the much greater event of the Resurrection.

John tells us that Jesus' mother was present (verse 1). Jesus' mother was also at the cross, and Jesus addressed her there in the same manner he addresses her here: He calls her *woman.* This term is a rather common designation Jesus used for women, including his mother (see 4:21; 8:10; Matthew 15:28; Luke 13:12). Although the term may seem rude, it is not unusual or disrespectful.

We are told that Jesus had been invited to this marriage along with his followers. Although Mary speaks to him about wine, he responds to her about his real mission (verses 3-4). The only way to understand this conversation between Jesus and Mary is to contrast Mary's goals with the goals of Jesus. Mary seems to signify purely human goals and human interests. Her maternal instincts are healthy in themselves—but they must not become an end in themselves. Human goals, however noble, must remain relative to God's will. And if human goals are always dependent upon God's greater will, they will be blessed accordingly (see Jesus' temptation in Matthew 4).

In any case, speaking as an Old Testament prophetic figure, he tells Mary that his time is *not yet come.* Much like an Elijah or Elisha, Jesus is about to change the whole meaning of the marriage "covenant" celebration. Similar to Elisha, Jesus will soon multiply the bread for all to eat (2 Kings 4:42-44). And similar to Elijah's (1 Kings 17:1-16) and Elisha's (2 Kings 4:1-7) miracles with oil, Jesus will change water into wine. But Mary asks her question on a domestic level; Jesus responds as one who is *in the beginning* with God.

Following this bi-level conversation (which is a typical characteristic of Johannine conversations), Mary tells the servants to do whatever Jesus tells them (verse 5). It is interesting that Mary's command somewhat echoes a Pharaoh's words about Joseph (Genesis 41:55). When there was a shortage of bread (a basic human need) during a famine, the Pharaoh directed the Egyptians to go to Joseph and do what he says.

We are told that water was stored in stone jars for Jewish rites of purification (verse 6). This apparently was a normal practice around a Jewish household.

Purification rites were Jewish religious customs that kept worshipers pure before God. It has already been carefully stated that John the Baptist baptized *with water* (1:26, 33) and the one who is to come will baptize with the *Holy Spirit* (1:33). The ingredients of purification rites—water baptism, wine, and the Holy Spirit—are the basis of the miracle Jesus is about to work.

Jesus now tells the servants to take the purification jars and fill them with water (verse 7). We almost get the impression they are filled to overflowing, suggesting the power and greatness of the Holy Spirit that is about to be released upon humanity (14:15-17). In this sense, Jesus takes the baptismal act of John the Baptist and changes water baptism into something far greater. Wine, of course, will be the drink shared at the Last Supper, symbolizing Christ's blood. Here, early in the Gospel, it already symbolizes a "new baptism" of purification that brings humanity in right relationship with God. This new baptism will be fully and eternally complete in Christ after his life, death, resurrection, and ascension. As we shall see, with the culmination of Christ's life in the ascension, Christ returns to the Father with our humanity ever representing us before him (Hebrews 4:15; 7:25).

Jesus instructs the servants to draw out some of the water now turned into wine (verses 8-9). The servants take on the future role of the disciples. It will be their duty to take the good news of the gospel to the people of this world. The steward of the feast does not know where this new wine has come from, but those who bring him the good news know. The steward calls the bridegroom. What an anticipation of the new marriage covenant in Christ! Suddenly this bridegroom is introduced into the miracle sign and complimented for saving the best wine until the last—the end time (verse 10).

Following the Old Testament, the *wedding feast* (and the *banquet:* Matthew 8:11; 22:1-14) implied messianic days. On the negative side, Hosea the prophet used a broken marriage relationship to symbolize how Israel had broken her *marriage covenant* with God. On the positive side, there are many affirmations of God holding to the covenant with Israel regardless of Israel's unfaithfulness. The covenant between God and Israel is portrayed as a potentially happy marriage that can produce joy and celebrations.

In this wedding feast, Jesus is all in all. He is the *bridegroom* and therefore the reason for rejoicing and celebration. He is the *new wine* that was saved for people to drink at the end—because he drank the vinegar of the cross (19:28-30; see also Psalm 69:21). He is the one who makes the wedding feast possible—and necessary. The Father gives the feast so that all can celebrate the sending of the Word to humanity. Christ is our purification so that the Holy Spirit can flow freely upon us, uniting us with the Father. He is the new covenant, the marriage that unites God and humanity together for eternity.

John ends his account by summarizing the event's significance (verse 11). This event not only *revealed* (made apparent) *his glory,* but his disciples *believed* (NRSV; NIV, *put their faith in him*).

Cleansing of the Temple (2:12-25)

The other Gospels also tell of Jesus cleansing the Temple. Perhaps the most striking difference in all four accounts is where this incident is placed in Jesus' ministry. In the other three Gospels, it is during the last few days of his life. John's Gospel tells of the incident at the beginning of his ministry. This gives the account different significance. In the other Gospels, Jesus cleanses the Temple just before he dies on the cross. Here he cleanses the Temple between the Cana miracle of new wine and the conversations with Nicodemus and the woman at the well.

The placing of this event at the beginning of John's Gospel emphasizes the new meaning of life in Christ. Under the old covenant, Israel came to the Temple, the place where God dwelled. Now Jesus cleans out this Temple, symbolically preparing it for the new marriage covenant and the arrival of the new temple: his humanity. Because God's Spirit dwells in Christ, the Spirit will dwell in Jesus' reconciled followers. John also tells us at the end of this account that the event had far greater importance in retrospect than it did at the time it happened. Nevertheless, this act did become an issue at Jesus' crucifixion (Matthew 26:61; 27:40; Mark 14:58; 15:29; Acts 6:14).

Just prior to this incident (verse 12), John tells us that Jesus returns home for a few days. His mother, brothers, and disciples are mentioned as his companions. Although this verse helps the transition from one important event to another, it may be that, if the writer was John the apostle, he is recalling an event that for some reason lodged in his mind.

We are told that Jesus travels to Jerusalem for Passover (verse 13). This was the major Jewish festival, the same festival during which Jesus would be crucified. In the Temple he finds many selling animals for sacrifice, and he finds moneychangers. The moneychangers were necessary because foreign money had the image of Roman leaders and was therefore unacceptable for paying the Temple tax (Matthew 17:27). Jesus fashions a whip out of cord and drives them out of the Temple (verse 15).

In the following two verses, Jesus explains the cleansing. He claims lordship over the Temple *(my Father's house)* and prophetically works another purification rite. In many ways this action is a prophetic act based on Old Testament sayings (Isaiah 56:7; Jeremiah 7:11; Zechariah 14:21). Later, for Jesus' disciples, this again indicated his messianic office and work.

Further, Jesus refuses to allow his Father's house to become a marketplace (verse 16). He is consumed by his *zeal* for his Father's house. Not only has Jesus become the new temple of God, but the new temple will not trade for human interests. His zeal is to do God's will.

Then John records that the Jews want an explanation for such a bold act (verses 18-21). Is there some sign that goes with this action? The conversation that follows between Jesus and the Jews is again in two different dimensions (as previously with Jesus and his mother). They do not understand each other. Jesus' sign is clear: If (When) you destroy this temple of my body *(this* referring to *my body,* not to their understanding of the Temple), I will raise it up again. This will be the sign.

Ironically, they completely miss the sign. The Temple was built in forty-six years, they respond; how could it be rebuilt in three days (the number of days Jesus will be in the tomb)? Then we are told that Jesus is really speaking of his body, and that even the disciples only understood this after the Resurrection. Several times now John has pointed out that the disciples do not see much more clearly than the Jewish authorities. This Gospel wants us to remember that, in retrospect, they saw very clearly.

By taking our humanity, Jesus becomes the true temple of God. But as Psalm 69:8 suggests (Jesus quotes Psalm 69:9 when he refers to his *zeal*), he also becomes *a stranger* to rebellious humanity, *an alien to my mother's children.*

Because Jesus is the true and everlasting temple, the one who alone lives a perfect life to the Father, he is *alien* to other persons. Yet all must worship God through him and in him and with him.

In the remaining verses of this chapter John gives us an indication that some are attracted to Jesus. We are told that many believed *in his name* when they saw *the signs* (verse 23). But there is no time wasted in telling us Jesus' response. He does not *entrust himself to them.*

Jesus seems to know that those who seek him are not sincere. Their hearts are not fully responsive. They perhaps say they believe, but Jesus knows differently. As with Paul (Romans 7), they want to follow Jesus' new way, but the flesh is unwilling. So Jesus sees their hearts. Perhaps they only want a sign—not God. Perhaps they want a signal and are not willing to stay with Jesus (1:37). We are not told what *signs* Jesus did, but we are told that Jesus would not *entrust himself to them.* Perhaps this would take more time, more fellowship, more teachings, and certainly his death, resurrection, and ascension when he would draw all to himself. He is an early indication of how many confront Jesus but do not understand and choose to delay full commitment. This sets the stage for the wonderful exchange between Jesus and Nicodemus.

§ § § § § § §

The Message of John 2

§ Human goals must always be formed in relationship to God's will.

§ God held to the covenant with Israel faithfully, despite Israel's unfaithfulness.

§ The Holy Spirit serves to unite us with God, after we have been purified through Christ.

§ § § § § § §

John 3

Introduction to This Chapter

Chapter 3 contains the well-known story of
Nicodemus, as well as more information about John the
Baptist.

Here is an outline of this chapter.

I. Nicodemus and the New Birth (3:1-21)
   A. Nicodemus is introduced (3:1-2)
   B. Earthly things and heavenly things (3:3-15)
   C. Salvation is universal (3:16-21)
II. Testimony of John the Baptist (3:22-26)

Nicodemus and the New Birth (3:1-21)

The previous three verses prepare the reader for this
section. Nicodemus appears as one who "sort of believes"
that Jesus was someone special. Here the conversation
takes place at night (verse 2). Nicodemus is attracted to
Jesus, but ironically he requests a meeting in the dark.
These circumstances remind us of an earlier verse, that
Jesus is *the true light* that gives light to all (1:9).

The conversation circles around the issue of faith.
Jesus, *the light*, speaks of radical change and total faith.
From the darkness, Nicodemus struggles to affirm what
Jesus is saying. On the one hand, the conversation
reminds us of the exchange between Jesus and Mary.
Nicodemus is speaking on a limited human level; Jesus
speaks on a grand divine level. In these verses the Gospel
continues to build upon the truth of God in Christ.

Nicodemus Is Introduced (3:1-2)

The chapter begins by identifying Nicodemus. The Greek word used to describe Nicodemus means *authority*, an official, a leading Jew, or possibly a member of the Jewish council or the Sanhedrin, the seventy leaders who ruled Israel from days of old (Numbers 11:16-20). So here is Nicodemus, one who "believes" but is not quite clear about things. He comes to Jesus and begins to question him.

He begins diplomatically. He calls Jesus a teacher (*Rabbi*, verse 2), using the same address as John's disciples (1:38). He further explains that *we* (probably other Jewish leaders) know that Jesus comes from God. His signs indicate God's presence with him. This is quite a cautious beginning for the conversation which is to follow. At this point, we get the idea that Nicodemus really understands what faith is all about. But as the conversation progresses, it becomes increasingly clear that he has a tremendous way to go—and we never find out if he arrives (although 19:39 suggests true belief).

Earthly Things and Heavenly Things (3:3-15)

Jesus' response begins with two important words. He says, *Amen, amen* (NIV, *I tell you the truth;* NRSV, *Very truly*) (verse 3). This term signifies Jesus' understanding that his forthcoming statement is vitally important. All of Jesus' statements throughout the four Gospels, preceded by *amen*, say something very significant about the kingdom of God. His use of the term in these verses is no exception. And here in John's Gospel, the term has a further importance. On the one hand, it introduces words that, in true Johannine fashion, carry double meanings (such as *dark, light, lamb,* and so forth). On the other hand, it introduces a conversation that will function on two levels—the level of humanity represented by the other person and the level of the divine represented by Jesus (as in the conversation between Jesus and Mary). Or we could explain this two-level conversation as two-directional: One direction is Jesus speaking from God to humanity; the other direction is from humanity to God.

In verses 3-10 both of these characteristics are easily recognizable. Jesus tells Nicodemus that he must be *born again* (NIV; NRSV, *from above*) to enter the kingdom of God. Jesus is speaking from God to humanity, explaining that a person must be redirected, repositioned, reconstituted toward God. This identifies a person as a citizen of the kingdom of God.

Nicodemus cannot understand this. His conversation is on the level of humanity. Nicodemus is thinking from humanity to God. He responds in human terms: How can this happen to an old person? We cannot be born again from our mother's womb. From the human side, this is impossible.

Jesus now deepens and broadens the conversation. Again using the term *truly,* he now relates *born again* to *water and the Spirit.* He clearly states to Nicodemus that he is speaking on a higher level, a level initiated by and dependent upon the activity of God's Spirit. Although John had baptized with water, Jesus now baptizes with the Spirit (1:33).

Throughout this Gospel and the book of Revelation, water is a symbol of fellowship with God through the Holy Spirit. In the book of Revelation, which is associated with the Gospel of John, statements about water and the Spirit abound. For example, God judges the earth by taking away water but allows the redeemed to receive water (Revelation 8:10-11; 16:4-5). The *lamb of God* leads people to the water of life (7:17; 21:6) and a river of life gushes from the throne (22:1-2).

Jesus continues his teaching in verses 7-8. Again he emphasizes being born anew. An alternative translation is "born from above." Nicodemus should not marvel at this, because it is God's work and not the work of humanity. God's work in human eyes is a miracle, a marvel. But from God's side, it is simply God's work. And with God, anything is possible.

The Greek word for *wind (pneuma)* also means *spirit.* The double meaning is significant. Following the witness of John the Baptist and the Cana miracle, water clearly signifies the Holy Spirit. So Jesus now explains that the *Spirit* of God moves and works where it will. But the emphasis is not on the mystery of movement but on the healing of the Spirit. Hearing the sound implies the *voice of the Spirit.* To be born from above, then, is to hear and be sensitive to the voice of the Spirit. We do not know where it comes from because it comes and speaks from God—not humanity. What a wonderful statement about the action of God's word for our salvation.

And Nicodemus voices the only human response to such a divine truth: How can this be? (verse 9). It is too marvelous for humanity—but not for God. Jesus responds with a little gentle prodding, emphasizing Nicodemus's status as a teacher as opposed to his inability to understand. The implication is that even a serious religious person may not hear the voice of the Spirit. Such a person may be too caught up in human religious activity and not take time to listen for the Spirit of God who freely moves toward us and for us.

Nicodemus, as a teacher of the law, would have been aware of Jewish teachings about the Spirit. The Spirit was to come in the last times (Isaiah 32:15; Joel 2:28-29). In some Old Testament passages the coming of the Spirit is connected with the sprinkling of water (Isaiah 44:3; Ezekiel 36:25-26). Perhaps these ideas inspired the thinking of Nicodemus after his meeting with Jesus.

The remainder of this section comprises a profound teaching of Jesus. The point has been made about hearing the Spirit of God. The Spirit unites humanity with God in fellowship. Now Jesus seems to be saying, Listen closely for the sound of the Spirit. Strain to listen in spite of your religious training. Allow the Spirit to freely lead you to God. Rely upon the Spirit and not your religious training.

In verses 11-15, Jesus further contrasts earthly and heavenly truth. Again Jesus begins with *Amen, amen. . . .* Using the terms *speak, know, testify,* and *seen,* Jesus portrays God's activity toward humanity. God is the Word spoken, and, as was done for John the Baptist (1:33), the Spirit gives us eyes to see, know, and witness. Those who do not receive the testimony are first Israel, represented by Nicodemus, and then humanity in general. And humanity cannot believe without the Spirit (verse 12). Because Jesus comes down to humanity, he lifts us up to fellowship with the Father, taking our humanity back to the presence of God (verse 13). As a Moses figure, Jesus the Word will lead all humanity to a right relationship with the Father when he is *lifted up* (verse 14) on the cross (see Numbers 21:9). Thus the Spirit's gift of faith is faith in him as the door to eternal fellowship *(eternal life,* verse 15).

Salvation Is Universal (3:16-21)

Now Jesus' statements are broadened to include all humanity. The verses above center on Israel. From verse 16, Jesus speaks on a level that far surpasses the old covenant. The new covenant in Christ is for all—all the universe. Nicodemus now fades from the scene as we hear Jesus speak of far-reaching universal truths.

Jesus begins with a grand statement. Here is the good news of Christianity succinctly stated. Jesus states that God first loved the world, and acted toward it. Notice how the verse begins with God's action and states that God came to the world in general. Only then comes the personal emphasis that whoever believes shall have life. In this manner God came down to us and will lift us up, uniting us forever with the divine. This is God's self-giving and self-sacrificing love that acts. God's Word acts. Now for those who believe because they hear the Spirit, eternal life is assured.

God's action is an action of love. The Son did not come to condemn us. What a positive statement about the world. We are not condemned, but saved. The term *world* (*kosmos* in Greek) refers to the entire universe of created things. In this sense, the world is the theater of history.

Belief in this personal Word of God to the world is restated in the remaining verses. The imagery of light is again employed. To be out of the light is to be condemned (verse 18). Judgment has occurred by the light. Now we must choose—simply because the light has come. Evil deeds are a sign of not choosing the light because the *sign* or deeds get in the way of God or eclipse God. But if we hear the Spirit bearing witness to the Word of God, we will more and more seek the light in response to God (verse 21). This will bear witness that we have chosen the Son when the Word of judgment comes to the world. Here we find in a few verses the new meaning of life.

Testimony of John the Baptist (3:22-26)

Jesus has been talking to Nicodemus about a right relationship between God and humanity. From the imagery of new birth, the Gospel turns to the final testimony of John the Baptist. And this important little section precedes Jesus' conversation with the woman at the well. The one who baptizes with water is meaningfully placed between these accounts.

We are told that Jesus leaves Jerusalem (verse 22). He goes out into the countryside, probably in the Jordan valley somewhere to the north and east of Jerusalem. The purpose for which he goes to the Jordan valley is important, and is often overlooked. We are told that he goes there to *baptize*. Jesus' baptizing work would have a different meaning from that of John the Baptist. John himself is causing a mild religious revival by encouraging people to repent because God is drawing near. After he privately identifies Jesus to his disciples, John continues to baptize. Jesus, on the other hand, who John said would baptize with the Holy Spirit, must have a deeper meaning and purpose for his baptizing of people. The relationship between the baptisms of John and Jesus must have caused some discussion among Jesus' followers for many years afterward.

Jesus' work of baptizing would have at least three important meanings. First of all, it is a further sign that Jesus' ministry is underway. We often tend to think that Jesus' ministry was launched with quickness and a sense of immediacy. But his baptizing work indicates that his ministry was more slowly evolving, as he responded to God's will, doing a work that had to be done. There are other signs, miraculous in nature. But here Jesus labors away at a more mundane task, launching his ministry of reconciliation.

Second, Jesus' baptizing ministry anticipates his command to the disciples that they baptize the world (Matthew 28:18-19). Throughout the Gospel accounts, what Jesus does reinforces what he commands his disciples to do. This is true with regard to prayer, healings, teachings, and so forth. (See, for example, Matthew 9:37-38; Luke 10:1-16.) Now the disciples have an example. Although they will not understand this example until after Jesus' death, here is Jesus doing what he will command his disciples to do later on.

Third, Jesus' baptizing of people would have to be different from the baptizing of John. Perhaps this is why discussion arises over Jesus' work in relation to John's baptizing. John is offering a baptism of repentance. Jesus would be baptizing people into his work of reconciliation between God and humanity. Because of Jesus' birth, baptism, and new ministry, the Kingdom has arrived. Thus Mark tells us that Jesus comes proclaiming, The time is fulfilled, and the kingdom of God is at hand;

repent, and believe in the good news (Mark 1:14). But we would also have to assume that either people do not understand Jesus' explanation of his baptizing or he does not fully explain its meaning—as evident in his actions and teachings in relation to the disciples.

We are also told that John the Baptist is still baptizing (verse 23). There would be no reason for him to stop. Jesus' ministry is unfolding slowly and will be misunderstood. So John continues to work. We are given two comments about his labors. We are told in an almost humorous manner that he baptizes where there is much water—absolutely necessary. Then we are told that people do come to him—because he has not yet been put in prison.

Then a discussion develops between John's disciples and a Jew (verse 25). The reference is possibly to a Jewish authority who may have been questioning what was meant by John's baptism. The Jews had certain purification rites or ritual washings that were undertaken prior to meals, at the end of a journey, at the beginning of the day, and so forth. Also, various groups like the Pharisees and the Essenes practiced continual washing and purification rituals.

The general thrust of the discussion is uncertain, but it causes enough controversy to stimulate John's disciples. They come to him and ask point-blank, What is the relation between you and Jesus of Nazareth? It is worth noting that John is rightly called *rabbi*, or teacher, by his followers, and that John is reminded how he *testified* about Jesus. Perhaps the growing popularity of Jesus adds to their discussion. Apparently more are going to Jesus than to John, and the disciples of John want an explanation. The implication is that they sense a greater truth in Jesus because of his popularity.

John then gives a beautiful response to the misdirected discussions of the disciples (verse 27). John throws their attention back to God. It is not the people who go to Jesus that make him great. It is not the witness of John or the interest of his disciples that gives him importance. Rather, everyone (including John's disciples) has been given a purpose or way of life by God. John's particular task is to be a good signpost. He is called to direct their attention to the One of God—and give them a lesson about themselves in the process.

Following these words, John appropriately restates his calling and work. He reminds them that he is not the *Christ* (verse 28 NIV; NRSV, *Messiah*). He knows his place. He is subject to the one who is to come. He is not the head of the new Kingdom (or church), but is subject to the Christ, the true head. He knows fully what he has received and been given from heaven.

Now comes a host of metaphors. The *bride* is the new Kingdom (or church). The *bridegroom* is the Christ. The *friend* is John himself. The bridegroom's *voice* is God's Word speaking to humanity the words of love, forgiveness, and reconciliation. *Joy* comes with all of the above because the Christ puts us right with God. John is using an Old Testament truth (Isaiah 62:5; Jeremiah 7:34) to witness the marriage or covenant contract between God and humanity as they come together *in Christ.* As Israel of old, the church must be true to the covenant that binds us to God in the Christ.

Then John the Baptist tells his disciples what this all means. The Christ must be allowed to increase. The Kingdom must come. What counts is not John's witness, but the truth of Christ.

The remainder of John's testimony is almost voiced as a self-witness on behalf of the messiah. John testifies that the Christ comes from God—from *above* (verse 31). John is pointing to God's spoken Word breaking into our world. This Word comes right from God. It is carefully spoken from God to humanity in a manner we can hear—it is spoken in the vernacular. Hence it also belongs to the earth. Without perhaps fully understanding what he is saying, John witnesses to the messiah as one who is fully divine *(above all)* and fully human *(of the earth).*

Now John seems to say a word about himself. He tells what he has received from God, and yet no one seems to understand what he is saying. But some are going to Jesus, and these receive Jesus' statements.

Then the work of the Holy Spirit is stated (verse 34). Two truths are held closely together here: uttering the word of God, and the full measure of the Spirit. The Spirit has one purpose: to engulf the Word of God that it may be heard and believed and responded to. Hence, faith and belief are gifts of the Spirit, activated when the Word is proclaimed and heard.

Then comes a dramatic summary of what has been said. The Father/Son relationship is one of binding love. It is this holy, divine love that overflows to all who accept the gift of faith from the Spirit and believe in the Son. This entire work of salvation is God's.

§ § § § § § §

The Message of John 3

§ As the concluding section of chapter 3 indicates, to *see life* is to enjoy the same covenant relationship with God that is first a truth between the Father and the Son. To turn away and refuse the gift of faith is to harden one's heart and enjoin the *wrath* of God.

§ God's wrath is not a personal attack by God upon the unbeliever. Rather, God's wrath is the result of running away or distancing oneself from God.

§ If to live is Christ, and to die is gain (see Philippians 1:21), then rejection of the Spirit's promptings and the Word of God in Christ can only result in a person's flight into darkness—away from the light. To not choose Christ is to choose the opposite. This is what John's Gospel calls *God's wrath.*

§ § § § § § §

John 4

Introduction to This Chapter

This chapter tells of the dramatic encounter between Jesus and the woman of Samaria. The second part of the chapter contains a healing miracle. John 4 may be outlined as follows.

I. The Samaritan Woman at the Well (4:1-42)
   A. Introduction (4:1-6)
   B. Jesus asks for water (4:7-15)
   C. Jesus is a prophet (4:16-26)
   D. The disciples return (4:27-30)
   E. Jesus teaches the disciples (4:31-38)
   F. Conclusion (4:39-42)
II. A Sign of Life's New Meaning (4:43-54)
   A. Introduction (4:43-45)
   B. The healing (4:46-54)

Introduction (4:1-6)

In order to introduce this account, the Gospel explains how Jesus comes into contact with this woman (verses 1-6). He has recently left Jerusalem for the Jordan valley. Now he leaves the Jordan valley of Judea, north of Jerusalem, for his home region in Galilee, farther north. The reason seems to be the Pharisees. Jesus is suddenly generating more religious interest than John the Baptist, even though Jesus' disciples are doing the baptizing—no doubt by his commission. So Jesus leaves this region for the north. Because Samaria is en route, he and his baptizing disciples pass through that region.

These verses tell of a significant shift in Jesus' ministry. Prior to this time, he has been baptizing people who come to him. Now we are told that his disciples have already begun to do this work (verse 2). As a result, Jesus' ministry now shifts from one of doing baptisms to one of teaching, proclamation, and miraculous deeds.

John explains that Jesus *had to go through Samaria* (verse 4). This would not really be necessary, assuming Jesus is simply traveling to the north with his little band of followers. Perhaps Jesus anticipates meeting the Samaritan woman and therefore chooses this route. But theologically this is an important encounter, because it reaffirms what was discussed with Nicodemus: that the messiah has come to redeem all humanity, not just the Jews. The incident explains that the messiah is to come from the undiluted southern kingdom of Judea.

The little town mentioned here is called Sychar. This is probably a reference to the ancient city of Shechem, now a small village to the southeast of the city of Samaria, and forty-one miles north of Jerusalem. It is only a stone's throw from Jacob's well.

More important, Shechem has great religious significance in the history of Israel. This was the first city Abraham visited as he migrated south (Genesis 12:6); Joseph was buried here (Joshua 24:32); it was here that Jacob gave land to Joseph (Genesis 48:22); Joshua renewed the covenant at Shechem (Joshua 24); Rehoboam was crowned king here (1 Kings 12:1); and when the northern tribes revolted, the city became the capital of the northern tribes (1 Kings 12:25). So Shechem became a symbol of northern rebellion and was an appropriate place for Jesus to explain how the messiah was to come from Judah in the south and not Samaria.

Another important factor helps set the scene. As noted above, this was the place of Jacob's well. This well was known as a good place for water. It would have been a deep hole, possibly one hundred feet deep. It would have been difficult to get water from such a deep shaft. The well would have been covered by a stone or large rock. Jesus either would have sat on the ground near the well or he would have rested on the stone covering the well, waiting for his disciples to return from town with supplies (verse 8). We are told he was tired—humanly exhausted from his journey. This is an important comment. This Gospel has already emphasized his equality with God (1:1-5, 14). Now we hear of his very human nature. Finally, we are told it was the *sixth hour* (NIV) or *noon* (NRSV). This is the exact time of Jesus' crucifixion when he also asked for water, but from the cross (19:14, 28).

Jesus Asks for Water (4:7-15)

In the first part of the exchange between Jesus and the Samaritan woman, Jesus initiates the conversation. The woman is surprised not so much at Jesus' question but at his willingness to speak to a Samaritan. The Jews disliked the Samaritans because they claimed to be the chosen nation, and they had refused historically to worship in Jerusalem. (This separation goes back to the rebellion following the death of Solomon in 722 B.C.) Eventually, the Northern Kingdom intermarried with other nations and thereby lost its Jewish religious purity. The people were hated by the Jews of the south. So it is only natural that this woman should voice surprise at Jesus' question.

Jesus attempts to help her understand his identity (verse 10). First of all, he shifts the conversation from water in general to the special water of his own personage. The Son is God's gift. Jesus implies that she, like all humanity, is in need of God's gift.

We also find here an indirect reference to prayer. Jesus tells the woman that if she only knew the situation, she would merely have to ask and God would give. Prayer through Christ, the living water, can never be void and fruitless.

The woman continues the conversation from her perspective, oblivious to the meaning of Jesus' comments. But she does now call him *sir,* or Lord. She sees Jesus as a mere person, who has no means to draw from the deep—almost divine—well of living water. She certainly does not understand him as the Word of God, the light of the world, the very one who is far greater than Jacob (verse 12).

As the conversation continues, Jesus contrasts the two levels of their exchange. He indicates that earthly water is not satisfying. But water from heaven is absolutely the opposite, being everlasting and fully satisfying. And once it is received, it becomes a *spring,* or producer of water within, leading to a fruitful life everlasting. The meaning is that once Christ puts us right with God, this will be a continual work.

The woman begins to sense something deeper going on in their conversation. Almost intuitively, she requests some of this water (verse 15). She has moved from curiosity to a deeper request. Here in a capsule is humanity's spiritual journey in relation to the Christ.

Jesus Is a Prophet (4:16-26)

Jesus, fully knowing the situation, tells her to fetch her husband. After her negative response, Jesus tells her spiritual biography: She has had five husbands, and Jews allow only three. She is a sinner. She has made mistakes. She is immoral. She has not been fully committed to a basic truth in life, that is, relationships. She has been in and out of covenants, both spiritual and carnal. Like the Samaritans, she has not been faithful.

The woman responds that Jesus must be a *prophet* (verse 19), one who has special divine knowledge. Then she introduces a topic that would be of interest to a prophet. It is stated in the form of a question/statement.

She seems to be asking, "Is it true? Is your insight really from God? Or are we to expect prophetic figures from this mountain in Samaria?" Jesus responds to the woman with some powerful statements about the one true God (verses 21-24). The true God of Israel is not the god of Baal. Each verse introduces a theme or truth about the true God of Israel. The *hour* (NRSV; NIV, *time*) is this Gospel's reference to the time of God's glory—an hour of which Jesus is well aware (12:27; 16:25). Jesus also now suddenly begins referring to God as *Father,* the Jewish family name for husband. This name for God is personal and loving, better translated *daddy.* Thus salvation comes by way of the Jews (verse 22). Only through God's chosen people is knowledge of God possible. All others worship what they do not know.

The kingdom of God is present now (verse 23). The *is now* means a new form of worship. This new worship refers back to the living water that opens the way to the very being of God the Father. This is real worship, in spirit and in truth. This worship means an inner change that is caused by the living water as it cleanses the inner person. Real inner communion with the Father means a true spiritual relationship. God is spirit because God relates to humanity in an inner relationship, bestowing the Holy Spirit upon the children of God through Christ the son (14:16). The other writings associated with John also state that God *is love* (1 John 4:8) and *God is light* (1 John 1:5). Together the three terms, love, light, and spirit, identify God as one who acts toward humanity.

In verse 26 Jesus comes right to the point. The Samaritans expected a prophetic figure, not a messiah. But the woman, sensing a deeper truth, introduces the Jewish expectation of a messiah. Jesus' answer is direct, with holy overtones. He virtually answers, "I am he." Jesus seems very willing to state his identity to the woman of Samaria, perhaps because the title *messiah* did not carry such political meaning as it did to the south in

Judea. In the south, the title was directly associated with David and kings.

The Disciples Return (4:27-30)

The disciples now return from town. They are amazed that Jesus is speaking with a woman. Probably out of respect for Jesus and the general situation, none dare voice their thoughts.

Immediately the woman goes off and becomes a witness to Jesus (verses 28-29). She is so keen to tell others that she leaves her pitcher, signifying her earthly cares and concerns. Her witness is put in the form of a question: Can this be the Christ? She seems to believe—or she would not have hurried to town. The only manner in which others will come to know and believe is to come and meet him face to face. They cannot trust her testimony alone. They must meet him. Like John the Baptist, she points to the *living water.* Her testimony is such that they do come and see for themselves.

Jesus Teaches the Disciples (4:31-38)

Meanwhile, a conversation begins between Jesus and his disciples. Here again the exchange takes place on two different levels. The disciples tell their teacher to eat so he will be refreshed and strengthened (verse 31). But Jesus explains that he has food—meaning his strength comes from fellowship with, communion with, and doing the will of the Father. This food they do not yet fully know.

Jesus then uses what is possibly an old proverb as a deeper commentary on their conversation. The disciples were on an errand to get food. Jesus speaks of the arriving Kingdom in terms of harvesting food. Four months was the traditional period before the harvest. But in contrast, there is now no waiting. The harvest is here.

The reapers are the disciples, or the church, who will labor in the work of God's kingdom and are blessed *(wages)* by rich fellowship with the Father. The sowers are the Old Testament church who labored to plant the seed. And Christ is the seed that produces the bread, the bursting grains, the lush harvest of the Kingdom.

Conclusion (4:39-42)

The final section is a conclusion to the episode. Many from the town respond to the woman's testimony (verse 39). Much like the first disciples, they abide with him and fellowship with him over a period of time. Jesus stays with them for two days, and many come to believe (verse 41). The townspeople's final statement to the woman summarizes the real meaning of the entire passage. It is because they actually meet Jesus—like the woman of Samaria—that they come to know, understand, and believe in him. Jesus becomes the seed planted here among the Samaritans. Because he gives them living water, the harvest is now ready. The prophetic history sowed the seed—the reapers are about to begin their labor. The Kingdom has come!

A Sign of Life's New Meaning (4:43-54)

Jesus has previously been associated with new wine and living water. Now a physical healing sign occurs as a confirmation of Jesus' identity and purpose. This is the second sign Jesus performs. Jesus heals by his spoken word. In fact, he speaks words from a distance to a young lad's father—a method of healing that Jesus is about to perform for all humanity. This particular healing event crowns Jesus' Temple cleansing, his conversations with Nicodemus, and his teachings to the Samaritan woman.

Introduction (4:43-45)

This section begins with three transition verses that move Jesus along on his ministry. He and the disciples now leave the Samaritan woman and the people of her little village, continuing on their journey north to Galilee. But there appears to be a problem; the second and third verses in this passage seem to contradict each other. Even though it is said that a prophet has no honor at home, Jesus is welcomed to his home district of Galilee.

Two possible explanations exist for this problem. First, verse 43 appears to be more of a local proverbial saying. At a time when there were itinerant preachers and numerous religious groups (John the Baptist, the Qumran community, the Essenes, and so forth), it is not surprising that such a proverb would be popular. Second, those who rejected him could be a reference to several groups. This phrase could be referring to Israel as a nation, the religious authorities in Jerusalem, or those in his home town of Nazareth. It certainly could be said that Jesus is heading back home for retreat and rest after his activities in Jerusalem and Judea. But his reputation is building. When he arrives in Cana, he is approached by someone who needs help.

The Healing (4:46-54)

The person who seeks his help is an *official* whose son is seriously ill (verse 46). Because his son is close to death, he literally begs Jesus for help. The Greek noun used for *official* suggests royalty or a court official (it is less likely that he was a soldier). Perhaps this person was a local court official appointed by King Herod. And perhaps he was at the wedding celebration in Cana when Jesus turned the water to wine. But upon hearing that Jesus is back in the area, he comes to beg Jesus' help.

Jesus responds to his request with a statement about *signs and wonders* (verse 48). Wonders and signs can distract from the truth of God. Jesus apparently wishes to correct any possible misunderstanding of what is about to happen. He wishes the truth of his person and message to stand out.

But the official has faith. Like the woman of Samaria,

he calls Jesus *Lord* or *Sir,* and simply requests his help. He asks Jesus to *come down,* stating metaphorically what Jesus in fact has done—come down from above in order to heal humanity, who is close to death. In this sense, the word for *child (paidon)* takes on significant meaning. The term means *small child* and has overtones of *God's child,* one having an undeveloped understanding.

Jesus' response is direct and exact. But suddenly the *child* is called a *son* who *will live.* The phrase seems to be full of meaning. In the biblical sense, God cares for believers who are sons and daughters of the Father because Christ is their brother. The result is life!

This life has a double meaning in John's Gospel. It means both recovery from sickness (2 Kings 8:9) and coming back to life after death (1 Kings 17:23). Because the man believes, he is able to go on his way with the assurance that everything is somehow going to be all right.

The official begins his journey home. His trip to Capernaum from Cana would have been about twenty miles, and it would have taken more than one day. Hence we are told that his servants meet him en route and give him the good news that his son is indeed living, and not dead. When he asks the hour of recovery, he is told *the seventh hour* (NIV; NRSV, *one in the afternoon).* Seven is a number implying divine perfection, and may suggest the perfect healing that occurred. We also should recall that John records a total of seven miracles or signs that tell of Jesus' true identity. The actual time of the seventh hour would be 1:00 P.M.

As a result, the father and his house have faith in the person, Jesus. Jesus had warned him not to simply see the sign or dwell on the wonder which was about to happen. He was encouraged to see beyond—to see Jesus, the one who gives life. This he does. And we are told that this is the second sign Jesus does in Galilee—the first being the water turned into wine.

§ § § § § § §

The Message of John 4

§ Jesus is the living water who quenches human thirst for God.

§ Jesus releases the spirit of God upon humanity.

§ Through Christ and the Spirit, humanity spiritually communes with God.

§ The harvest is ready among those beyond Israel.

§ Jesus is God's Son and he is reconciling God to humanity.

§ Miracles emphasize Jesus' identity and mission.

§ Through Christ, "little children" can become "sons and daughters" of God.

§ § § § § § §

Introduction to This Chapter

In the next five chapters, Jesus is placed against the backdrop of Judaism. Jesus is directly related to four Jewish festivals. Although the first feast is unnamed, it is either Pentecost or the New Year festival. (If the first verse is understood to mean that Jesus was required to celebrate the feast in Jerusalem, then the festival is probably Pentecost.) The other feasts mentioned are Passover (6:4), Tabernacles (7:2), and Dedication (10:22). The writer of John's Gospel has a definite purpose in mind throughout this section. Jesus is presented as the fulfillment of the meaning of these feasts. He is understood and presented as the essence and the completion of all Jewish expectations.

Chapter 5 may be outlined as follows.
   I. Healing on the Sabbath (5:1-18)
  II. Teachings About Healings (5:19-47)
      A. Relationship between Father and Son (5:19-29)
      B. Testimony about the relationship (5:30-40)
      C. Jesus judges the Jews (5:41-47)

Healing on the Sabbath (5:1-18)

We are told that Jesus goes to Jerusalem. On this occasion, a healing marks Jesus' arrival in Jerusalem. This would be an appropriate act by Jesus at the New Year festival and it would be an appropriate act for Pentecost because of the sabbath controversy that follows. The healing would suggest that the arrival of Jesus, the *new Word*, brings a new time. This new time is characterized by healing, restoration, and wholeness. The sabbath discussion that follows the healing is a tension between the old time and the new time or the old law and the new law.

This healing event (the third sign) has unusual characteristics. Jesus performs this healing in Jerusalem, on the sabbath, at a major Jewish feast, an in an unusual manner. At this high religious occasion, Jesus fulfills all of these unusual characteristics. He is the Word of God who comes in an unusual manner (the incarnation); he comes to his own, to Jerusalem, the place where God dwells; and he redefines the Jewish sabbath, becoming the new sabbath.

This healing takes place at the *Sheep Gate pool* (verse 2). This was an entrance to Jerusalem near the Temple also known as Bethesda. It was a gate where sheep were brought into the Temple for sacrifice. This pool has been identified and excavated. The five porticoes, or colonnades, were arranged with four on the outside and one in the middle. The pool was quite large—about 200 by 300 feet—with steps descending down to the pool in the corners.

We are told that many disabled people are around the pool (verse 3). The explanation for this, given in the next verse, is not included in all manuscripts. It was the popular belief that an angel periodically came and disturbed the waters. The first person to enter the water after this disturbance would be healed. During a key Jewish festival, the moving waters would probably be expected.

One person in particular is at the pool on the day Jesus passes by. He has been ill for thirty-eight years—a lifetime! He is crippled. Like a "sinner," he cannot function normally. Jesus then asks him if he would like to be healed (verse 6). We can note four things about Jesus' question: (1) Jesus speaks to the sick person first. He initiates everything by first coming to him. (2) His coming to this person demands a response. It is a direct and serious question expecting a response. It is a direct and serious question expecting an answer. (3) As the story unfolds, it becomes clear that Jesus' question has overtones of spiritual healing or being put right with God. (4) Finally, Jesus' question in the context of a Jewish festival suggests a new time for humanity. This is how we can be healed—in and through Jesus, the lamb of God.

The man's answer is the answer of all humanity. Again Jesus is addressed as *Lord*. The man has no one to help him be healed. Jesus' response is instantaneous. The man is called to his new life in Christ by taking up his pallet and going to work. This he does immediately.

The Jewish authorities see the man carrying his pallet. So they ask him, from the perspective of the old sabbath or the old time, why he is doing so. It was forbidden to carry things, including beds, on the sabbath. The cured person immediately bears witness to Jesus. *The man* told him to carry his bed. The Jewish authorities want to know the identity of this man. But the healed person is not certain. It is crowded, and we are told that he knows Jesus only by sight.

This man is very much like Jesus' disciples. He does not fully understand who Jesus is or the deeper meaning of his healing. Also, the Jewish authorities shift the meaning of the event. They are concerned about Jesus' identity for one reason: He has broken the sabbath law. The healing is of little importance. The issue for them is Jesus' blatant breaking of the sabbath law when he commands this man to take up his bed and walk.

On their next meeting (verse 14), Jesus tells the healed man to sin no more because he is *well*. Not only is this statement made in the Temple (the place where God dwells) by the lamb of God, but we are told it is Jesus who finds him. Jesus again makes the initial contact. If the man responds (with gratitude) in his new spiritual state to God's grace, nothing worse will befall him—he will never be separated from God.

Now the man becomes a greater witness for Christ. He goes and gives testimony to the Jews. He tells them exactly who it was who healed him. Then we are told that the Jews begin to actively persecute Jesus.

Jesus' first response to this beginning Jewish hostility creates greater tension. After he gives an initial statement (verse 17), the Jewish authorities become more angry because of his explanation. The Jews are furious about his breaking the sabbath. Jesus explains that even though the law is broken, *my Father* is working out his will for all humanity. As with Jesus' other conversations (Mary, Nicodemus, the woman at the well), there are two levels evident. Jesus speaks from God to humanity; the Jews are speaking from humanity to God.

Relationship Between Father and Son (5:19-29)

Jesus now gives a more formal answer to the Jewish authorities. He begins again with the words *Amen, amen,* designating the importance of what he is about to say. The intimate relation between Father and Son is stated with wonderful clarity. The Son can only act as the Word of the Father. Jesus' seeing the Father indicates their deep relationship. No one knows and sees the Father except the Son. Thus the action of the Son is the action of the Father, and vice versa. This relationship is based on love (verse 20). And greater works will result than the healing about which the Jews have complained. The greater works are because of the love between the Father and the Son—a love that is even now spilling over to all creation.

Jesus then turns to raising the dead and giving life (verse 21). In the midst of Jewish hostility that will lead to his crucifixion, Jesus speaks of a new life that will include a new sabbath, new law, and a new "temple." Because he will be the first to be raised up, all will be judged *in Christ* (verse 22). Hence the Father will not judge; only the Son who gives life will judge everyone. By trusting in the Son and the Word of the Father, honor is given to the Father and the Son. So we cannot honor the Father except through the Son. There is no other way to God.

Then a summary statement is given. Salvation comes by hearing God's Word and accepting (believing) the Father who sent the Son (3:16, 36).

Then again we read the words *Amen, amen* (verse 25). The *dead* who will *hear the voice of the Son* are the spiritually dead who are out of relationship with God (Ephesians 2:1). Hearing is again identified as the way to life—hearing and listening to God's Word spoken in Christ. What is life? The Father has life and the Son has life or eternity (verse 26). Hence the son is the *Son of man* and the *Son of God* in that he is God become humanity, the first Son among many sons and daughters. All will be judged through Christ, even those already dead. Christ is the key, the center, the purpose to all things—to the entire universe—past, present, and future (see Daniel 12:2).

Testimony About the Relationship (5:30-40)

In the four verses above, Jesus speaks of how the Father gives to the Son. In the next ten verses, Jesus speaks of how the Son can do nothing except what he receives from the Father. The same must be true for all Christians. Those who seek the Father's will through Christ and in the Spirit live in truth. This was a common emphasis of Jesus (see, for example, Matthew 26:39; Luke 22:42).

In general the Father loves the creation. In particular God embraces humanity among all creatures, moving freely toward us. Because Christ is God's Word spoken to humanity, what Christ has is from the Father (verse 34). Salvation does not come from humanity, but from the Father. John the Baptist makes this clear by his testimony. John was a lamp pointing to the arrival of

Jesus. But now we see something far greater. Jesus accomplishes greater things than John the Baptist—evident already in the miracle of the water and the wine and the healing of the lame man. These *greater works* (NRSV; NIV, *weightier*) are only signs of the greatest work of all, the saving of humanity. These already-accomplished works are a sign of Jesus' true identity.

Likewise, the Father bears witness to the Son (verse 37). The Jews have not heard his voice nor have they really seen his form. Metaphorically, Jesus is saying that the Jews never really knew God. But now Jesus witnesses to the very character and being of God—as God "tabernacles" right before their eyes. His listeners do not hear his Word. They have gone so far as to trust in written words alone. They have forgotten about the God behind the Scriptures. Their Scriptures have eclipsed the living God. Now the *living Word* is before them and they cannot see it (verse 40).

Jesus Judges the Jews (5:41-47)

In this final section, Jesus turns more specifically to his Jewish audience. He begins by saying that he *receives glory* not from humanity but from God (verse 41). The glory is everything the Son receives from the Father. Thus salvation comes from God through the Son to humanity. Humanity cannot save itself—as the Jews were attempting to do by fulfilling the law. Rather, the good news originates with God and is accomplished (the fulfilling of the law) by God.

Those who do not trust in the Word, the Son of God, do not know the love of God. Because they are out of relationship with God, they do not have the love of God within their hearts. Hence, unlike John the Baptist (1:33), they cannot hear God's voice and do not recognize the Word of God spoken in Christ (verse 43).

So what does Jesus say to the Jews? Jesus says

point-blank that he will not condemn them (verse 45).
Jesus comes to give life, not death. He brings good
news—not bad news. Jesus then says that Moses accuses
them. But how? They stand accused by Moses in two
ways: First, they choose to live under the old law and not
the new law of Christ. They refuse to hear God's Word.
Second, they cannot keep the law. The law was meant to
get their attention. Only Christ can properly fulfill the
law—and this Christ does for all humanity.

Jesus concludes by stating his completion of God's
Word begun with Moses. Moses received God's law;
Jesus fulfilled God's law. In this way, Moses wrote of
Jesus the Christ. Humanity cannot fulfill the law. Thanks
be to God that the law was fulfilled by God's Word who
came in the flesh. Hence Jesus concludes that if you do
not believe Moses, you will not believe and understand
what Jesus speaks and acts in his earthly life (verse 47).

§ § § § § § §

The Message of John 5

Jesus fulfills the meaning of the occasion, regardless of
whether John is referring to a Pentecost or New Year
festival. By performing a miracle on the sabbath, he
becomes the healing truth of a new sabbath that will be
completed at his resurrection. This will make him the
real *life-giver* and *judge*.

The Jewish authorities would have understood these
claims as an attempt to usurp the powers of God and
claim divinity. By these claims, Jesus asserts the
beginning of a new time (the New Year festival) or that
he represented humanity's new historical relationship
with God (the Pentecost festival).

§ § § § § § §

John 6

Introduction to This Chapter

This section records Jesus' attending Passover. This festival was held in the spring of the year. As noted with the previous festival, Jesus' activities and teachings are appropriate to Passover. Jesus feeds the large crowd, supplying life's bread; walks on the sea and quells the storms of life; and teaches about his identity as the bread of life. For the Jews, Passover centered on two general themes: God's deliverance of Israel in the *past* (through Moses) and God's promised deliverance of Israel in the *future* (through the coming messiah). Into this situation Jesus arrives. Through his work and teachings, he redefines Passover.

Chapter 6 has three parts.

I. Feeding the Five Thousand (6:1-15)
II. Jesus Walks on the Sea (6:16-21)
III. Jesus the Bread of Life (6:22-71)

Feeding the Five Thousand (6:1-15)

The transition verses are important at the beginning of this chapter. Geographically, Jesus crosses over the water. We are reminded of the Israelites crossing the Red Sea.

Because of what has occurred in chapter 5, Jesus has a significant following. Jesus healed the diseased, and seeing the signs the people followed him. And now further healing signs are about to be given that suggest continued health maintenance—but only in Christ. (This is the fourth sign.)

Jesus goes up the mountain with his disciples (verse 3). This reminds us of the opening verse of the Sermon on the Mount in Matthew 5–7, or the Sermon on the Plain in Luke 6–7. Something very important is about to happen. The stage is set. Jesus is at the center of the scene. The disciples are next in order, gathered around Jesus. Then come the masses.

The feast of Unleavened Bread (Passover) intimated many significant things for the Jews. This was the bread that sustained the Israelites during their deliverance from Egypt (Exodus 12). In like manner, Jesus is about to become the *unleavened* (sinless) bread that will sustain all humanity during their deliverance from sin and rebellion. The unleavened bread of Passover is the bread of *affliction* (Deuteronomy 16:1-8). As it helps the Israelites remember their past, so Christ the true bread will help humanity remember their daily dependence upon God.

Jesus sees the crowds *coming toward him* (verse 5), and immediately inquires about their basic needs. His overriding concern is for the sustenance, upbuilding, and general maintenance of those who would follow him.

Jesus' question to Philip is exact: Where shall we buy bread, so that these people may eat? The question is full of Old Testament overtones and parallels when compared with Israel's murmurings in the wilderness (Numbers 11). Moses asks God a similar question (Numbers 11:13). In Moses' situation, the people grumbled, as do the Jews after Jesus refers to himself as the *bread from heaven* (verses 41-43). Jesus teaches about *manna* (verse 31), referring to the Moses incident. In both cases, bread is the sufficient substitute for flesh. Finally, there is a reference to "possible" fish (Numbers 11:22) and to the supplying of fish by the little boy in John's Gospel (verse 9). The parallels seem to suggest that in the past God supplied Israel's needs. But now, in Christ, humanity's needs are supplied completely and forever.

Then we read that Jesus is simply testing Philip. The emphasis of the verse is on Jesus. Although Philip is *encouraged* or tested in his faith, Jesus knows what has to be done. He knows his mission. He knows the work he has to accomplish. Philip, thinking on a different (materialistic) level, as with Nicodemus and the woman at the well, simply responds by saying the cash is not available (verse 7). The amount of money referred to by Philip would be equivalent to two hundred days' wages, an amazing sum.

Then Andrew (*Simon Peter's brother*) introduces a wonderful change in the setting. It is not unimportant that a *boy* has a lunch—a lad similar to the one healed earlier (4:49). The servant of the bread of life is a young lad or a child. The innocence, wonder, and trust of the child are the very characteristics associated with those who would follow Jesus. Further, barley loaves are the food of the poor (the *poor in spirit*), those who need to be healed. Dried fish is a normal food, although eventually a fish became the sign of the church. As the Gospel states, Andrew is not enthusiastic about the advantage of this little lunch in relation to the masses of hungry people.

Jesus takes command. He tells the disciples to have the people sit down—perhaps not an easy task considering the masses and possible confusion. In the normal Jewish manner, only the men are numbered. Undoubtedly, on the basis of the lad himself, women and children are present. How Jesus gets the lunch is not stated, but we can assume one of the disciples (probably Andrew) asks the boy if the master or *rabbi* can make use of his little parcel of food.

Jesus gives thanks, or says a prayer over the food, and the people are filled. The Greek word used for Jesus' *thanks* is *eucharistein,* or eucharist. This later came to mean the sacrament of the Lord's Supper. Hence, the breaking of the bread and drinking of the cup at the Last Supper carry the meaning of *thanksgiving, blessing,* and *communion.* The fact that the people who *came to Jesus* were filled implies the sufficiency of Christ. He is the fulfilling of God's free choice of love and fellowship with humanity. Nothing more is needed.

The disciples are then commanded to gather up what remains so nothing is lost. This gathering up is similar to the gathering of the manna in the wilderness (Exodus 16:16-20). But unlike the manna of old, this "manna" (Christ) in the "wilderness" (of this lost world) must not be lost. The mission must be fulfilled.

In the fulfilling of the mission, when the son or lamb is sacrificed, God's costly grace is not to be wasted or mocked or to return to him void (see Jesus' instructions to the seventy, Luke 10:1-12). The disciples fill twelve baskets. Here is a reference to the remnant of Israel or the twelve new tribes of Israel, the body of Christ.

Jesus is immediately identified as a prophet (verse 14). Perhaps he is identified as a Moses-type prophet (see verse 31) who will do great things for the people of God. They so misunderstand his mission that they seek to make him king (verse 15). So Jesus withdraws to a *mountain* for meditation and communion with the Father. The sign of the feeding was meant to explain how *the one* (his identity) feeds the man; how this *one act* (his mission) in time is an act for all humanity for eternity. Jesus, then, is the bread of life that overcomes the troubled world.

Jesus Walks on the Sea (6:16-21)

We are told that evening has come (verse 16). When the *light* of the world is present, great things happen: Water is changed to wine, living water is offered, healings occur, a little bread feeds thousands. When the *light* of the world withdraws to go to the Father (13:13), evening comes.

The disciples go down to the sea, board a boat, and

begin to cross over the water. It is dark, and Jesus had not yet come to them. Here is a wonderful description of the church: a group of people, having known the light, setting out in faith to cross over in the darkness, trusting in the ship or the church of Christ to carry them to the other side. This entire section is symbolically rich.

The terms *water* and *sea* carry important biblical meaning. From the Genesis Creation accounts, the earth or order arises out of the chaos of water. Noah is spared the devastating flood the engulfs the earth in chaos. God holds back the flood of waters at the Red sea and the Israelites cross the Jordan in order to enter the Promised Land. In this context, Jesus is the new living water that redirects the world of rebellion and chaos. The dark waters of chaos are replaced by the calm waters of God's truth.

So here we find Jesus' disciples out on the sea of chaos. The sea becomes violent, treacherous, and ever more dangerous (verse 18). They work hard; they row continually (verse 19). They are only about halfway across the lake, perhaps a bit farther, when something happens. They see Jesus walking on the waters, and he is drawing near to them.

The disciples are terribly frightened. They are not exactly sure about Jesus, though they surely have their ideas. When they see him walking on the water, their uncertainty about him probably intensifies. But Jesus reassures them with powerful words: *It is I; do not be afraid* (verse 20). It is his person that assures them, not their impressions of him. It is Jesus who must eventually count for the disciples, not some image or comforting thought.

The incident concludes with two events. Jesus comes into the boat and they immediately reach the shore. John explains the first event from the disciples' side. They are glad *to take him into the boat*. In the midst of the storm, we get the impression of big sighs issuing from the disciples.

When Christ enters the disciples' boat, they have a taste of the end time. They immediately reach safety. To be *in Christ* is to have a foretaste of what will be and already is.

Jesus the Bread of Life (6:22-71)

These verses tell how the people sense something miraculous is going on in their midst. There is only one boat, and Jesus has not entered that boat. Jesus has gone elsewhere; he has ascended to the Father in spiritual fellowship. So the disciples *had gone away alone.* The people first look again at the miraculous place where the feeding occurred, where they ate and were satisfied. No one is there. So they go off in search of Jesus (not in search of the boat or the disciples).

When they find him *on the other side,* they ask him how he got there. Jesus' response is a lengthy teaching on the meaning of who he is and why he has come (verses 26-34). First he warns them that they should seek him for *who he is* and not because of signs and miraculous events.

He is the bread and he satisfies all who feast on him. The food of this world perishes—as do those who eat the bread of this world. But the *Son of man* offers the opposite, that is, imperishable food that gives eternal life. The word *seal* is found often in the book of Revelation. It generally refers to the *sealing* of God's people, protecting them from the horrible events of the end time—from the sea of chaos, destruction, and separation from God. As used above (3:33), it indicates the divine seal of Christ, who binds together for eternity God and humanity.

The people who have sought him out respond with a question. What *works* should they be doing? They speak first of their own human works. God's works are twofold: (1) that they believe—faith is a gift of God; (2) *in whom* (NRSV; NIV, *the one)* he has sent. But the people are unable to follow what Jesus is saying.

As with Nicodemus and the woman at the well, John reports a two-level conversation. The people want only a sign—the very thing Jesus warned them about at the beginning of their discussion. They then relate Jesus' feeding of the masses to God feeding the Israelites in the wilderness. In Jesus' time, the expected sign of the messiah was the offering of manna as of old. These Passover pilgrims want the sign of the *true messiah* (verse 31).

Jesus returns to his initial emphasis. He explains that signs and ancient personalities are not God. Only *my Father* can give you *true bread from heaven* (verse 32). This bread must come from God if it is to give life. Their response to this proclamation is to request the bread— always or forever.

Now Jesus turns them again to his person and mission. All human thirsting and hungering are satisfied by Christ. He who comes to Christ, led by the gift of faith, will be fully satisfied. But they cannot believe because they want a sign, they want some proof (verse 36). They want to see something miraculous. Ironically, they are looking at the miracle of the incarnation and cannot see it!

The Father gives all humanity to the Son. In his humanness, Christ will cast no one out. He dies for all and reconciles all to the Father. This is his mission, to do the will of the Father who sent him. None of those given to the Son by the Father (through the gift of faith) will be lost, but they will be raised up in the final day of judgment (verse 39). This theme is then restated with the emphasis on the Father's will. Those given by the Father to the Son are the body of Christ, the ship of believers, who travel across the waters of chaos. These believers will be lifted up on the far shore.

Now the masses begin to hear more clearly what Jesus is saying. But generally they do not like what they hear. They begin to murmur and complain, as did the Israelites before Moses in the wilderness. But they murmur here for different reasons. With Moses, they wanted secure and permanent food. With Jesus, they have this; but they take offense because he is making himself out to be equal with God. How can the son of Joseph say he has come down from heaven (verse 42)? Jesus tells them of their murmurings. This is something they do among themselves, and not with God in mind.

Jesus then tells them that faith is a gift from the Father. They can only understand him and accept the gift of faith if they rely upon the Father and not on their own resources—on their own religion. Because they accept the gift of faith and feast on the bread of life, death cannot harm them. The bread of life is far greater than the manna of old. The bread of life comes from above, not from the earth.

Then Jesus concludes these remarks by identifying himself as the bread of life. He is living bread that comes from the living Father to humanity. He concludes, the bread *I will give for the life of the world is my flesh.*

Again, the Jews do not comprehend what Jesus is saying. Now Jesus changes, deepens, and broadens the explanation, by way of his association between himself as the bread of life and his flesh. He also introduces his blood as a means to life. By means of his blood and flesh, he will raise up those who feast on him. Again he states that this is not his own work, but he is sent by the Father and comes down from heaven.

The disciples, the inner twelve, the new Israel, complain. They complain that it is hard to accept what Jesus is saying. They too apparently complain among themselves, and Jesus responds to their murmurings—just like the murmurings of Israel in the wilderness. He tells them what they will eventually see: the Son ascending *to where he was before.* He will ascend to the place where God dwells. Without Jesus, there would be no possible relationship between the Father and humanity.

In the final section, the Twelve and the others are separated. Many who appeared as followers abandon the ship (verse 66). Jesus then challenges the Twelve, and Peter acts as a spokesperson witnessing to Christ's person and work. Lest they rely on their own strength, Jesus assures them that he first chose them. He knew them so well that he was aware that one would abandon him in the end (verses 70-71).

During this festival Jesus will die on the cross. Thus it is important to recall that the old Passover celebrated God's deliverance of Israel and the eventual coming of a messiah or savior. This is the context of Jesus' deeds and teachings which now establish a new Passover celebration. As God acted toward Israel in the past, so now God acts specifically toward all humanity in Christ the messiah, the word of God. His body and blood will become the real eternal Passover bread or food of reconciliation between the Father and humanity. He alone overcomes the dark chaos and evil. Eternal life is Christ because of who he is and the mission he completes.

§ § § § § § §

The Message of John 6

In this Passover feast, the emphasis falls on Jesus as
the bread of life and Jesus' power over chaos. At the
previous Passover, he cleansed the Temple. On the next
Passover, he will offer himself as a sacrifice for the many.
So we see a movement from getting the *temple* (of his
body) *ready* to now establishing the new element (the
unleavened bread) and rationale (defeating the seas of
chaos), to finally reconstituting this entire Jewish festival
that celebrates God's deliverance of Israel.

During this second Passover, Jesus is established as the
bread of life. He is a prophetic Moses figure of the past,
and manna, the shewbread that was expected to be a sign
of the new messiah's arrival. He is the bread provided by
God to reconcile humanity to God. But he is also the
future bread of life (the bread of the Lord's Supper). He
is the new Passover that will allow those present (the five
thousand) and all pilgrims of the festival to feast on him.
They will rely upon his soon-to-be-accomplished work
(the next Passover) of reconciliation.

§ § § § § § §

John 7–8

Introduction to These Chapters

For the next 153 verses, Jesus is involved with the Jewish feast of Tabernacles (see the commentary on 1:14). This is a major pilgrimage festival that was celebrated in Jerusalem for eight days in the fall of the year (September/October). Also known as the Festival of Booths or Ingathering, it required that pilgrims actually dwell in booths or branch huts in the vineyards. Because God had provided for the people of Israel during their wilderness wanderings, the people now combine thankfulness for these past blessings with thankfulness for the current fall harvest.

This festival is also known as the Feast of God (Leviticus 23:39), celebrating the dedication of Solomon's Temple (1 Kings 8) and the Torah (Deuteronomy 31:10-11). Perhaps the attention given to this festival is related to one tradition that suggested the messiah would "come out" or arrive during the feast of Tabernacles.

John 7–8 may be outlined as follows.

  I. The Feast of Tabernacles (7:1-52)
 II. The Woman Caught in Adultery (7:53–8:11)
III. Jesus the Light of the World (8:12-59)

The Feast of Tabernacles (7:1-52)

In the first section of this chapter, Jesus has an interesting conversation with his disciples. The Jewish authorities are seeking to kill him. He is too outspoken against their sacred beliefs and traditions. Nevertheless, his *brothers* encourage him to go south, down to Judea, so that his *disciples* can see his great works. *Brothers* possibly refers to Jesus' relatives—brothers, cousins, and so forth (based on Jewish usage). The brothers make this suggestion even though they do not believe (verse 5).

The typical Johannine two-level conversation is evident in Jesus' response. His *time* (Greek *kairos* means much more than mere calendar time) has not yet come. Though he does great works now, these are only indications of the great healing work that he will do on the cross and in the Resurrection and ascension. Because his brothers are of the world, their time is always present.

Jesus travels to Jerusalem privately for the feast (verse 10). He is not attempting to fool the brothers. He is attempting to keep his works from displacing his greater mission. The Jews aggressively look for him by asking the wrong question: Where is he? (verse 11). John contrasts the question of the Jewish authorities with the muttering of the people. The people are rightly interested in *who* he is and not in *where* he is (verse 12). But the people do not speak openly, and the confusion about Jesus remains.

In the next group of verses, Jesus teaches openly. In the middle of the feast that celebrates the law and the Temple, Jesus teaches in the Temple (verse 14). The Jewish authorities are amazed and want to know where he got his education (verse 15). A Jewish education was a lengthy period of study under a good rabbi or teacher. So their question is, "Under whom did he study?" or "From whom did he get his insight?"

Jesus' response contrasts divine and earthly authority. In the prophetic tradition, Jesus bases his authority solely in God. He has no authority from this world, that is, from a rabbi. And if one is seeking to do the will of God, one will recognize whether Jesus' teachings are of God (verse 17). Jesus throws their questions back upon their own

74

religious faith. What do they really believe in, God or some earthly teaching of Scripture?

Now the people who seek to know *who he is* are offended at his statement that they seek to kill him (verse 20; see Mark 3:22). Jesus then refers to the healing he did on the sabbath (5:1-15). To work on the sabbath meant death, according to the ancient Jewish law. But the Jews practice circumcision on the sabbath (verse 22; *patriarchs* refers to Abraham, Genesis 17:10). Circumcision took place eight days after birth and sometimes had to be performed on the sabbath. Circumcision was the rite of removing the foreskin from the penis. It was a sign of the covenant that would ward off evil. Hence Jesus appeals for fair judgment because he healed the whole person and not just part of a person.

The people remain confused about Jesus. It is known that the Jewish authorities want to kill him because of his teachings and sayings. Yet nothing is done by the Jewish authorities—probably the members of the Sanhedrin. What are the opinions of the authorities? Are they giving silent approval? But then they reason that it is known where Jesus is from—Nazareth. At that time, a person was known by where he or she was from.

Jesus responds by contrasting earthly and heavenly places of origin. Jesus is not from where they think, that is, from Nazareth. He does not come of his own accord, but he comes from one whom they do not know, from God. He *knows* God, *comes from* God, and is *sent* by God (verse 29).

The authorities are offended. Could they have been tricked by God and not have been told openly and clearly of the messiah's arrival? Surely not! So they look for the opportunity to arrest him; but the right opportunity does not arise. Then the people reason further, could the messiah do more signs than this person? (verse 31; see Isaiah 35:5-6).

The next section again contrasts two levels of

conversation. It begins with the crowd again muttering, so the Pharisees take action and seek to arrest him. Then Jesus tells of his mission. Though he is with them for a while, he will be returning to the Father.

The remainder of this chapter now shifts to the last day of the feast (possibly the seventh day). Jesus begins by stating that he alone can quench spiritual thirst. Referring to the wilderness wanderings of Israel, Jesus now claims to be the rock from whom the spirit flows (verses 38-39), and people will be satisfied only in him (Numbers 20:2-13). *Water* signifies the Spirit (verse 39), and only Jesus can give the Spirit. Jesus now contends for the people (as Moses did) and prepares to send forth the Spirit because of what he is about to accomplish for all.

A significant part of this festival included water. During each morning of the festival, the priests would process to the fountain of Gihon near the Temple to secure a pitcher of water as the choir sang Isaiah 12:3. After they returned to the Temple through the Water Gate, the water was poured into a funnel and it went into the ground while the people sang Psalm 118:5 and the Hallel, Psalms 113–118. The water at this festival signified God's sending water for the future harvest.

These words impress some of the people. They begin to identify him as a prophet or the messiah. But in the end, they remain divided. Those who would arrest him want to know why nothing has been done. The officers testify and the Pharisees reject their testimony. Their argument is that the authorities reject him and the people are untrained in the Scriptures. Nicodemus then speaks up in a mild defense of Jesus (verse 50). But the authorities are adamant that Galilee is not the origin of the messiah. They do everything by the book. Nicodemus argues for his identity *(Who is he?)* rather than where he comes from.

The Woman Caught in Adultery (7:53–8:11)

This section is not found in the earliest manuscripts of John's Gospel. It is found in later manuscripts (fifth century) and in some later editions of Luke's Gospel. Because it is an attempt to trap Jesus and because it reflects his gentle and kind treatment of people, we can accept it as an account that comes from Jesus' life.

After the crowd breaks up following Jesus' previous teaching, Jesus goes out to the Mount of Olives—probably to pray. When he returns to the Temple the next day to teach once again, a dramatic situation unfolds. A woman who was caught in adultery is thrown into the midst of the people. Jesus is told to state her penalty, and they remind him of the Mosaic law (Leviticus 20:10; Deuteronomy 22:21). According to Jewish law, only a woman could be found unfaithful in marriage, not a man. As the rabbi or teacher, Jesus is expected to know the law of Moses, so they ask him a "test" question (verse 6). Jesus dramatically bends down and writes in the dust. This is the only record of Jesus writing.

Finally Jesus answers them after their continued requests. Apparently, much to their surprise, he paraphrases Scripture (Deuteronomy 17:7). Again he bends down and writes. Beginning with the eldest (or the most sinful), they leave. Jesus' questions to the woman suggests that true judgment comes as we stand before God, not humanity. And because of Christ, God is forgiving.

Jesus the Light of the World (8:12-59)

Following John's normal pattern of event and dialogue, we now hear some further teachings by Jesus as he speaks with the Jewish authorities. These sayings seem to be grouped together by John for this particular occasion. They explain how Jesus is the true meaning of the Feast of Tabernacles.

In the first section (verses 12-20), Jesus begins by

explaining his mission. He is the *light of the world* (see Isaiah 49:6). In the Temple court, great golden lamps were used to light the precincts during the feast of Tabernacles. This would seem to be an appropriate claim by Jesus. A deeper meaning is the pillar of light that led the Israelites in the wilderness (Exodus 13:21). Jesus is now the pillar of light who will lead his people through the darkness into the light of the Father. But the Pharisees, working on a different level, argue that one cannot bear witness to oneself. Jesus claims to be above such a limitation; he is from God and not from humanity.

Because Jesus is from God, he judges no one. Those of the flesh judge each other. But the messiah leads the way back to God. His task or mission is not to judge but to be the light that shows the pathway to God. Nevertheless, Jesus' judgment is true because it is God's judgment (verse 16). He is beyond, or the completion of (see Matthew 5:17), the law, the surpassing the law's limitations. If he is beyond the law, then where is his authority? His *Father* (verse 19)? Jesus claims equality with the Father as he stands near the Temple treasury or the Temple precincts (verse 20; see Mark 12:41).

In the next section we once again find two levels of conversation (verses 21-30). Jesus states that he is going away to a place they cannot come, referring to their hardened religious practices that buffer them from God. The Jews speculate that he will kill himself. The extremes of their positions are stated in the next verse. Jesus seeks only the Father's will; they seek their own will. The way they can seek God's will is to believe in Jesus—*that I am he* (verse 24 NRSV; NIV, *I am the one I claim to be*). The *I am* is a clear claim of divinity and oneness with God (Exodus 3:14). This inspires the Jewish authorities to ask the ultimate question: *Who are you?* Jesus' response here is difficult to translate, but can be rendered "From the beginning (I am) what I say to you." Jesus continues, stating that he speaks only the message he has heard from above, from the Father (verse 26).

The authorities do not understand him. This is the other level, the level of human comprehension. In particular, they do not understand his use of the term *Father*, a very unique term for God. Then Jesus combines all the key terms in his response to these officials. He refers to himself as the *Son of man* and as *I am*, and he refers to God as *Father*. Finally he assures them that anything he speaks is not his own.

Verse 29 beautifully unites ingredients that Jesus will encourage among his disciples: being *sent*, never being left *alone*, and doing only the Father's will. As a result, we are told that many believe in him (verse 30).

With those who believe in him, Jesus engages in a rather lengthy conversation. This conversation takes place between Jesus and some serious inquirers who are attempting a response to Jesus, and this all takes place during the great feast of Tabernacles. This conversation begins with Jesus emphasizing freedom (verses 31-33). Jesus is the *Word* that will make them disciples of the truth. The word of truth will make them free for God, and will not legally burden them as their religion currently does. Their response is that they in fact are free in Abraham.

Jesus tells them that their focus is too much on sin. They should focus their attention not on sin, but the Son of the household. But these believers are more concerned about Abraham (their father) than about the Son (who speaks of the fatherhood of God). Jesus points out a technicality they have overlooked. Abraham, in the tradition of the commandments, would have stood for no killing. Yet they seek to kill him. They then claim they love God the Father. Jesus responds quickly, then why don't you receive me? I was sent by God (verses 42-43). Then Jesus tells them that their current father is the devil, the leader of rebellion against God the Father, the author of murder and lies. Jesus cannot be sinful because he comes bearing the truth of the Father, yet they want to claim that he is sinful. Thus they cannot hear what he has to say.

Jesus' audience claims he is like the hated Samaritans: He has demons inside him. Jesus responds by continuing his claim of authority from God the Father. He honors the Father, the Father glories in the Son, and if people keep his *Word* they will never die or lose the presence of the Father.

The Jews are now convinced that he is demonic because everyone, including Abraham, has died. Again they ask the critical question: *Who are you?* His answer attempts to make the inquirers focus primarily on God the Father. It is the Father who glorifies the Son, and not the other way around. And even Abraham, their father, foresaw his coming (Genesis 12:1-8), because he believed God's Word and promise. This tense situation ends with Jesus claiming to be prior to Abraham (*before Abraham was* [NRSV; NIV, *was born*] *I am*), and their attempts to stone him in the very precincts of the Temple (verses 57-59).

§ § § § § § §

The Message of John 7–8

In this section, Jesus is understood and explained through the major themes of the Jewish feast of Tabernacles. Perhaps John had in the back of his mind the ancient tradition that suggested the messiah would come out of this festival celebration. The major themes are the following:

§ This festival was intended to bring all Israel together. In the same manner, Jesus is God's Word reconciling all humanity to the Father (Zechariah 14:16).

§ The pilgrims gathered in the holy city Jerusalem, the place were God dwelt in the Temple. It is in the Temple that Jesus teaches, heals, and debates his true identity with the religious officials of Israel.

§ The feast celebrated Israel's wilderness wanderings when God provided for their needs. Jesus is God's light who shines in the dark wilderness of life.

§ Jesus is the water of life who sends the spirit to replenish humanity.

§ This feast celebrated the harvest. Jesus is the beginning of God's true harvest reconciling the Father with humanity.

§ This feast celebrated the Torah, or the law. Jesus is the full and true wisdom of God, God's definitive word spoken forever to humanity.

§ § § § § § §

PART NINE John 9–10

Introduction to These Chapters

These two chapters are concerned with themes relating to the Feast of Dedication. They may be outlined as follows.

I. Jesus Heals a Blind Man (9:1-41)
II. Jesus and the Feast of Dedication (10:1-42)

Jesus Heals a Blind Man (9:1-41)

In careful contrast to the "blind" inquirers above, Jesus now gives sight to a blind person (the sixth sign). The man was blind from birth, and the conversation resolves around the cause of his blindness. The causes suggested by the disciples are theological or spiritual, not physical. Again Jesus focuses on God the Father, explaining that this particular case of blindness allows God to manifest divine truth.

Jesus does the works of the Father in the daylight because he is God's light to the world. So Jesus takes some clay and with his own spittle anoints the man's "spiritually" blind eyes. Thus, faith in the Father comes from the Spirit through the Son.

The man is told to wash in the pool called *Siloam*, or *Sent*. This pool was a water supply for the Feast of Tabernacles and a pool used for purification rites. The beggar man is transformed because he now sees. Although he is not recognized, he gives testimony about Jesus. The Pharisees investigate, only to discover that it happened again on the sabbath. They are in a quandary over what to do. He does great things—but he keeps breaking the sabbath! The official investigators bring in the parents of the man who received his sight. The parents, fearing the Jewish authorities, explain that he is mature and can give his own testimony. They prefer to keep out of it.

The seeing man is now interviewed once again. They press him to *give glory to God* and denounce Jesus. The underlying issue is clear: Who is Jesus? But the man can only testify to what he knows and what has happened personally to him. The man repeats his story but the Jews would *not listen* or accept his testimony. They mock and ridicule him. Then the man, with spiritual clarity and perception, states their problem and concludes that Jesus must be from God. But the man is treated like Jesus' disciples: He is cast out.

Then the healed man once again confronts Jesus. Jesus actually seeks him out and questions him, *Do you believe in me?* The now seeing man worships Jesus and we are given an explanation of what has happened. Jesus came to *judge* or be a *light* to the world, that those who are blind and have no light will see by this light. But those who think they see because they trust in the false light of religious perfection (or self-achievement) will be literally blinded by the light of Christ.

Then some Pharisees ask, *Are we also blind?* Jesus explains that persons who are blind do not trust in their own achievements— and therefore are not guilty about what they may have failed to achieve. But when persons claim to *see* apart from the light, they are relying on their own strengths and powers, disregarding the true light of the world. So they remain guilty or self-condemned.

Jesus and the Feast of Dedication (10:1-42)

Israel was heavily persecuted in the 160s B.C. by the Seleucids, one of three remaining segments of Alexander the Great's empire. In December 167, under Antiochus Epiphanes, the Seleucids desecrated the Temple altar. But led by a priest and his five sons, a rebellion broke out. One of the sons, Judas Maccabee, eventually reclaimed Jerusalem, and in 164 purified and rededicated the Temple and altar. This eight-day rededication became an established ceremony in Jewish history, also known as Hanukkah (1 Maccabees 4:50-51; this is the only Jewish festival not ordained in the Hebrew Bible). Hanukkah is considered a second feast of Tabernacles because it remembers God's providing for Israel during the many months they lived in caves while fighting against the Seleucids. These eight days are also known as the Festival of Lights, celebrating the rekindling of the Temple light that signified God's presence.

During the eight days of celebrations, the Jews emphasized at least two general themes. One theme explained the role of God as shepherd of Israel and Israel as God's sheep. The other general theme anticipated God sending a shepherd in the line of David to be king over the Jewish people.

Against this backdrop, John places Jesus in Jerusalem at the December Feast of Dedication (10:22). Jesus begins by appropriately teaching about sheep and shepherds (verses 1-6). He opens with common sense: The only way into a sheepfold is by the door. Any other entry is that of a bandit, a robber, a rebel. Then Jesus explains this more fully using several themes. The *gatekeeper* (NRSV; NIV, *watchman*) is God, who sends the Holy Spirit upon all who enter through the Son, the gate or door. Through the Spirit, the sheep recognize and hear the voice of the shepherd. He calls each by name—he knows each one personally. He leads them out of the wilderness (or the caves) into the presence of God, beside the cool waters. He goes before them and protects them.

The next section elaborates on these themes even further (verses 7-18). Jesus patiently begins again. *Amen,*

amen: He explains that *I am the gate.* Others have come claiming to know the truth or be the truth, but they are the ones who attempt to enter the sheepfold by another way. Jesus is the only way to the Father. By communing with him, believers can go *in and out,* continually communicating with the Father. The shepherd comes to the sheep—they do not find him. But not only this, the shepherd remains the daily door to the Father.

Those of this world have a different plan. The *thief* operates out of self-interest. As a result, robbers tend to destroy the plans of God. But Jesus has come and is the door to green pastures, the door to salvation. He will die for the sake of his sheep—this will be the beginning of their new life.

There are other sheep. These are Gentiles who have yet to hear the shepherd's voice. But they will soon hear because there can be only one flock and one shepherd. The shepherd gives his life to the Father, but in giving his life to the Father he fulfills the Father's will on behalf of humanity. Thus he will again take up his life because the Father loves the Son and the Son loves the sheep.

The Jewish authorities have difficulty with Jesus' teachings (verses 19-21). One group argues that he has a demon and the other group senses that something greater is going on here.

Jesus is still in Jerusalem at the December feast of Dedication, and he is walking in the Temple. The divided Jewish authorities question him in a matter-of-fact style. *Are you the Christ?* (verse 24, NIV; NRSV, *Messiah*). Jesus claims that the truth is before their eyes. Because they will not accept the gift of faith, only his sheep in the fold are eternally secure. This is all from God, and he and the Father are one (verse 30).

Again Jesus' life is threatened (verses 31-39). They want to stone him. Jesus' response to their action is to once again state how he has done good works *from the Father,* not from himself or from humanity. The Jews think he is human and claims to be equal with God. Jesus' true identity is the issue. Jesus quotes Psalm 82:6 in his own defense (verse 34). This hymn tells about a vision the psalmist experienced. He saw a council of gods that ruled the world. But because they ruled unjustly, the God of Israel judged them. Their actions betrayed them. So Jesus responds to the Jewish authorities, stating that Scripture is truthful, and it states that the actions of these lesser gods are not acceptable. Jesus explains that here is a reference to other gods in your own Scripture, and it states that their actions were wrong. So now you will stone me because I said *I am God's Son?* (verse 36). They are astonished at his boldness and try to arrest him once again.

This time Jesus leaves Jerusalem. While he is across the Jordan, the testimony of John the Baptist is again stated (verse 41). Many believe, because he fills the role John has described. He also fills the role that he has just presented the Jewish authorities at the feast of Dedication: He taught great things and he did wonderful works.

§ § § § § § §

The Message of John 9–10

Jesus explains that not only does God the good shepherd come to the sheep in the person and word of Jesus, but God eternally covenants with the sheep.

§ Jesus is the new Davidic king who will make one sheepfold for all humanity.

Some further themes that John seems to imply are the following:

§ This feast celebrated the rededication of the Temple. Jesus now surpasses the Temple as the place where God dwells. He is God incarnate, rededicating all humanity for dwelling in right relationship to God.

§ Between the desecration of the Temple and its rededication, the Jews depended upon God to supply their needs. Now God supplies the shepherd, the light, the water, and the bread for the chosen people living in the caves of wilderness as they await his return and final purification.

§ This feast celebrated freedom in worship. Now in Christ all are free to enter the sheepfold through the door.

§ Finally, one tradition states that the light in the Temple burned for eight days—hence the festival of lights. Jesus is the new light that shines in the darkness and will never be quenched.

§ § § § § § §

John 11:1-54

Introduction to These Verses

This is the second longest narrative in all four Gospels. The longest narrative is the account of Jesus' death. Although this grand event centers on Lazarus, it seems to flow out of and help interpret Jesus' resurrection. In this manner, the resurrection of Lazarus confirms and establishes Jesus' mission and identity. Looking forward, it is precisely his power over death that allows him to redefine and reconstitute the Passover festival. Looking back, this event is a fitting sign that Jesus is the new focal point of all major Jewish festivals. For the early Christian community in Ephesus, the recalling of this event must have held significant importance.

Here is an outline of John 11:1-54.
  I. The Story of Lazarus (11:1-44)
     A. Introduction (11:1-4)
     B. The death of Lazarus (11:5-16)
     C. Jesus arrives in Bethany (11:17-27)
     D. Jesus speaks to Mary (11:28-37)
     E. Lazarus is raised (11:38-44)
 II. Jesus' Death; Lazarus's Resurrection (11:44-54)

Introduction (11:1-4)

This event takes place in a small community called Bethany. The village of Bethany is apparently known only because Mary and Martha are from this village—not because of Lazarus (although the current name of this village, El' Azariyeh, may derive from a variation of the name Lazarus). We know nothing about the person Lazarus (with the exception of verse 3 below). Lazarus was a rather common name during New Testament times and literally means *God helps*. But there is no indication that this meaning has any importance for John's Gospel.

Mary is identified in verse 2. This statement appears to be an editorial addition that clarifies this Mary as the same Mary who anoints Jesus' feet before his crucifixion. Also we are told that Lazarus is her brother. Mary and Martha send a message to Jesus: He whom you love is ill. As a result of this message, there have been attempts to identify Lazarus with the disciple Jesus loved (13:23; 19:26). However, the evidence is not very convincing. Although Jesus seems to be friends with Lazarus, no further information is known about their friendship beyond this verse.

Jesus' response to Mary's message anticipates what is to happen. Jesus speaks in accordance with God's plan, not human plans. In the perspective of the Resurrection, illness is not final. The light now shines in the darkness and it will not be overcome by death and darkness. The Father's plan is being fulfilled.

The Death of Lazarus (11:5-16)

Now the dramatic story unfolds. We are told first that Jesus loves Mary, Martha, and Lazarus. This statement is perhaps meant to reassure us that Jesus is hesitating to go immediately for a greater plan or purpose, that is, God's purpose. "Delays" and God's plan become an important theme in the early church (see 1 Corinthians 15; 1 Thessalonians 4:13–5:11; James 5:7-8).

After a two-day delay—possibly symbolizing Jesus' days in the tomb—he and his disciples begin their journey toward Jerusalem. Near Jerusalem he will give a sign of his own resurrection that will soon follow in the Holy City. These two resurrection events set off and indicate the meaning of the new Passover.

In the midst of these new beginnings, Jesus is warned by the disciples. Because he does the Father's will, and is the Son of God, his very life is threatened. Jesus answers the disciples with a practical question full of theological meaning. Do we not travel by the light of day?—by the light of the world? (verse 9). The sun's light keeps us from stumbling. But at night, the opposite is the result. The deeper meaning is that Jesus is the light. By his light we travel through life.

Once again we find two levels of meaning evident in Jesus' exchange with his disciples. Jesus calls Lazarus a friend and states that he *sleeps.* The disciples seem to think that sleep after illness is good. Jesus then tells them plainly that Lazarus is really dead. Even though Lazarus is dead, Jesus refers to him as a person. He explains that what the disciples are about to witness with regard to this person will comprise the basis of belief. Then Thomas, seeing only the danger involved in Jesus' going to Jerusalem and apparently not understanding Jesus' statements about Lazarus, says, *Let us . . . die with him* (verse 16).

Jesus Arrives in Bethany (11:17-27)

This section dwells upon Jesus' conversation with Mary and Martha. By the time Jesus arrives on the scene, Lazarus is dead *four days.* An old Jewish tradition said that the soul stayed near the body for three days. After that time, there was no hope of life—a tradition that most likely stemmed from real-life situations.

Bethany is identified as being two miles from Jerusalem; it was close enough to associate the coming event with the Holy City. Apparently many come from Jerusalem to comfort the sisters during their mourning. When Jesus arrives, Martha goes out to meet him and Mary sits in the house. But later it will be Mary who anoints Jesus' feet (chapter 12).

Martha's statements are the words of humanity. *Where*

have you been? and *You can do all things.* There has been a delay and the result is death. At the moment, and humanly speaking, things are in a disastrous state. From a divine point of view, God's plan of salvation is eternal and is being worked out. Jesus then speaks the words of comfort that comprise the Christian message to all who suffer loss: They will *rise again* (verse 23).

Now we find Martha's statements in reverse. Because you can do all things, he will rise, but after a delay on the last day (verse 24). But, Jesus responds, it is happening now. He explains that he is the true *resurrection and life.* Belief in him means life even though we are dead. Jesus is speaking in anticipation of his victory over sin and rebellion. Then Jesus asks Martha if she believes him. Her response is confession of his true person and mission. The phrase "come into the world" suggests the continual working out of God's master plan in Christ, with the Resurrection and ascension yet to come.

Jesus Speaks to Mary (11:28-37)

The next group of verses brings Mary into the picture. Jesus delays in coming, speaks with Martha, and now Mary. When Martha calls Mary, she does so privately, a wonderful commentary on the sensitivity between the sisters. Mary is perhaps more distraught, having suffered more emotionally over the loss of her brother. She seems to have needed time alone. The two sisters are a good example of different believers from diverse stations in life responding to Jesus the Christ.

When Mary hears Jesus has come, she quickly responds. She goes out to commune with him before he comes (again, suggesting the end time) to their situation of need, to the place where her sister already communes with him. Eyewitnesses from Jerusalem think she is going out to the place of the dead. They follow her. But instead of worshiping the dead, she worships the living, the Christ. Her statement reflects that of Martha: If you had not been away, everything would have been all right. Mary's confession reflects the future experiences of the church—and all believers. If Christ had not been away, if he had not ascended to God on behalf of humanity, things would be different. But he has gone away. He delayed for a reason. He delayed so people would come to believe.

Then Jesus sees the pain of Mary and the others. When he comes to know their suffering, the suffering of humanity, through his flesh, he is tremendously moved. The Greek could be translated, *moved with the deepest emotions*. Further, Jesus is *troubled,* almost angry (the same verb is found in Matthew 9:30 and Mark 1:43). Perhaps Jesus is angry at the suffering humanity endures as a result of evil and rebellion. In any case, Jesus is motivated to act. *Where is he?* mirrors God's question to Adam (and Eve) in the garden. *Where is the one dead in sin?* Jesus is invited to *come and see,* to come and see the cave of darkness and sin that holds the person he loved. Then follows a short, profound verse: *Jesus wept* (NIV; NRSV, *Jesus began to weep)* (verse 35). Those on the scene, Jews from the Holy City, Jerusalem, completely misunderstand his weeping. They think he cries merely for his dead friend. But some expect more. Some reflect the bitter taste of losing a friend and loved one. If he can do the other, why can't he do this, too?

Lazarus Is Raised (11:38-44)

Then comes the miracle. Jesus is again *deeply moved* (NIV; NRSV, *greatly disturbed).* This time he is not empathizing with humanity; he is boldly acting for humanity. He steps in front of the cave that resembles the one in which he will be buried. He commands that the stone barring his access to Lazarus be removed. Jesus boldly portrays his power over the grave—a power that will soon be evident in his own resurrection. Martha reminds him that there is a problem. She is disturbed, and attempts to distract Jesus by reminding him of the four days in the tomb and the expected stench. But Jesus can see only God's will.

The stone is removed. What a dramatic confrontation between the *light of the world*, the Lord of life, and the darkness of the world, death. As if to maintain his focus, Jesus does not first look to the darkness of the cave when the stone is taken away. He looks to the heavens and prays to God. This he does at his own death on the cross (Luke 23:46). Addressing God as *Father*, he gives thanks for what God *has done*. He states that this is a *witness* for those present. The witness is that he is not to be distracted from God and the divine plan for the creation in general and humanity in particular.

The time, God's appointed time, has arrived. With a loud voice Jesus shouts out the name of his friend, commanding him to respond.

Notice how Lazarus responds! He comes out, still bound with the signs of death, destruction, and suffering—bandaged and bound. His hands, face, and legs are restricted. Like humanity, he cannot heal himself; he cannot get free of his burdens. Jesus then commands the signs of darkness and death to *let him go*, just as he frees humanity eternally for God. This event is dramatic and full of meaning.

Jesus' Death; Lazarus's Resurrection (11:45-54)

This dramatic miracle is the height of all that Jesus has done up to this point in the Gospel. But the result is further polarization. Those who are with Mary are divided: Some believe and some are suspicious and unaccepting. This latter group go to the authorities and report what they have seen.

The Sanhedrin Council is convened to discuss the situation and the validity of the signs Jesus performs. The coming messiah is expected to give signs. But who is this Jesus? There seems to have been a good deal of confusion; they go on to discuss the possibility of Roman action against them and the Temple. Perhaps this suggests their interest in a political messiah; or it may suggest that the people are being misled. In any case, they represent human reflection on the universal question: *Who is Jesus?*

Then Caiaphas the high priest (see 18:13 for an interesting contrast) makes a prophetic suggestion. As is often the case in John's Gospel, his suggestion has a double meaning. It has clear practical meaning because it will get the Jewish authorities off the hook and curtail any danger from aroused Roman officials. Yet it has tremendous unknown theological meaning because Jesus will die to reconcile all children (or humanity) to God. This suggestion seals Jesus' earthly fate, a fate previously determined by God for the salvation plan of history.

With the Jewish plot established, Jesus does not first seek confrontation. Rather, he immediately seeks communion with God in an isolated setting. He and the disciples go to the country *near the wilderness (NRSV; NIV, desert),* the place of prophetic preparation.

§ § § § § § §

The Message of John 11:1-54

This event is the focal point of the Gospel. It is the crowning action of all that has gone before—of Jesus' teachings and healings. Here is the climactic seventh and most nearly perfect sign that has been building since the opening verses.

From here, things move in a different direction. Jesus begins carefully instructing and preparing the disciples for his absence. He redefines the Passover for Judaism and all humanity. There is a plan of salvation; there will be delays, but God's plan is being worked out. The new direction begins here at the tomb of Lazarus. This is the "watershed" sign.

Jesus even tells the meaning of this event before it actually happens. In this sense, Lazarus's death is a preview, a window, a foretaste of Jesus' death. In Jesus, death itself will be destroyed. It is asserted here that he has the power to do just this.

§ § § § § § §

John 11:55–12:50

Introduction to These Chapters

Passover has arrived. This is the third Passover recorded in John's Gospel (2:13-25; 6:1-14). The third Passover seems to symbolically express Passover perfection. Certainly at this Passover things are quite different. This Passover is preceded by the raising of Lazarus from the dead and followed by Jesus' steady movement toward his own death and resurrection. In this context Jesus announces that *the hour has come for the Son of Man to be glorified* (12:23). The remaining half of the Gospel deals with this critical new Passover hour.

Now Jesus is no longer just the radical rabbi teaching new things in the Temple precincts (10:23-24). This hour means that he now becomes the *Lamb of God* (1:36) who takes away the sins of humanity. With this chapter John concludes the dramatic transition to Jesus as the center of Passover. But these events also mark the final and full rejection of Jesus by the Jews. Up to this point, they are undecided, they are forced to decide who Jesus is. Their rejection is complete, crucifying and burying the one who some thought might be the messiah. This chapter affirms John's earlier statement in 1:11.

Here is an outline of this section.

    I. Jesus Anointed in Bethany (11:55–12:11)
   II. Jesus Enters Jerusalem (12:12-19)
 III. Greek Interest in Jesus (12:20-26)
 IV. Final Public Teachings (12:27-50)

Jesus Anointed in Bethany (11:55–12:11)

The last verses of chapter 11 move the scene from the raising of Lazarus to the third Passover's events. (The synoptic Gospels tell of only one Passover; thus the question has been raised as to the length of Jesus' ministry, that is, whether it was three years or only one year.) At the first Passover, Jesus cleanses the Temple in Jerusalem (2:13-25); during the second Passover he teaches and performs miracles in Galilee rather than Jerusalem (chapter 6); now at the third Passover he is the center of attention—the talk of the pilgrims journeying to Jerusalem.

Many went up from the country to Jerusalem (verse 55). Jerusalem was the center of Israel and Judaism. Regardless of where one was in the country—north or south—one always *went up* to Jerusalem, the center of the religious and cultural life of the Jews. The best estimates suggest that Jerusalem was a city of about 25,000 under normal conditions. During major festivals, such as Passover, probably close to 100,000 pilgrims swelled the city to the point of bursting. Many pilgrims would have come early in order to purify themselves for Passover (2 Chronicles 30:17-18; Acts 21:24-26).

Many who attended this particular Passover had heard about Jesus. There appears to have been discussion as to whether he would come to the feast. The Jewish authorities, meanwhile, sought to arrest him. Perhaps they were simply seeing the right opportunity. If Jesus were to attend Passover, only two types of circumstances would keep him from the Jewish authorities: Either he would remain hidden—if that were possible—or he would become the center of attention. Both circumstances seem to have been evident during Jesus' Passover attendance.

Jesus begins his journey to Jerusalem because his *hour has come* (12:23). He first goes to Bethany, near Jerusalem, where Lazarus was raised from the dead. This is an important symbolic visit, emphasizing his power over death in the face of his own death—for others. Jesus arrives about a week (six days) before Passover. A dinner or banquet is prepared, and although it is mentioned that Lazarus is in attendance, he is not the reason for the dinner. Although not clear to the people attending Passover, it is the person, Jesus, who is central to the activities and the reason for the festive occasion.

Then we are told that Mary anoints Jesus' feet (verse 3). Mary is the one who prefers listening to Jesus (Luke 10:39), and Martha is the more energetic one. This preference for listening to what Jesus has to say inspires her to anoint Jesus' feet. The washing and anointing of his feet is in appreciation for where Jesus has trod and where he will go. The perfume or ointment is probably made of myrrh (called *nard*). Matthew's Gospel mentions this as a gift given by the wise men at Jesus' birth (Matthew 2:11). This spice was also used for burial preparations. Here Mary is wise because she unknowingly prepares Jesus for his journey to the cross.

Mary wipes Jesus' feet with her hair. This action has tremendous Old Testament significance. Esau (Genesis 25:25), Absalom (2 Samuel 14:26), and Samson (Judges 16:17-22) are remembered in part because of their hair. In light of the Old Testament, Mary's act is a priestly and prophetic sign confirming Jesus' imminent work of reconciling God and humanity.

The entire *house* (or creation) *was filled with the fragrance* of his anointing. This sweet-smelling incense and Jesus' coming sacrifice would be pleasing to God.

But there is resistance to Jesus' work. Judas complains that they should be thinking of the *poor* and not of Jesus (verses 4-5). Judas has things out of order, however. The poor are not helped by ignoring Jesus; in fact, the poor are helped by first giving attention to Jesus and then living out a life of real and active worship before God. To not live out such a life is to not be a witness, a disciple.

Jesus' protection of his followers is well portrayed in verse 7-8 (see Mark 14:3, where the jar is broken and all the perfume is used). Guarding his true followers, Jesus implies that what perfume she has left can be used to complete his enbalming after his sacrificial death. The remaining perfume will assist his followers in relying upon Jesus after the ascension, after he returns to God in order to represent all humanity (John 17).

Crowds then seek Jesus because of the Lazarus sign (verse 9). The circumstances needed for Jesus' arrest remain elusive for the Jewish authorities. So they decide that Lazarus, the living sign, must also be terminated. He is getting too much attention for Jesus (verses 10-11).

Jesus Enters Jerusalem (12:12-19)

Now comes the story of Jesus' Passover entry into Jerusalem. The news has spread: Jesus is coming to the Holy City. His reception is mighty indeed. The palm branches signify many things. This tree provided fruit to eat (dates), a drink from its sap, branches for house roofing, and material for weaving baskets. The palm tree was also found around oases (Numbers 33:9), the only places of water in the desert. This was a very hardy tree (Psalm 92:12-14). Jesus could be said to symbolically fulfill all of the above characteristics.

The people shout a variation of an Old Testament psalm (Psalm 118:26). This was not an uncommon theme to those who would make their pilgrimage to Jerusalem for Passover. But as the words are shouted to Jesus, they take on a different meaning. Jesus *comes in the name of the Lord* rather than one who is " blessed by the Lord as he comes."

The additional statement, *king of Israel*, is a commentary on the paraphrased psalm. The "king" was a messianic figure who would come and do great signs.

Jesus then takes the initiative in fulfilling Scripture (see Zechariah 9:9). The disciples are ignorant of this sign, an embarrassing admission by those who are to become apostolic leaders in the church (verse 16). This only becomes clear in retrospect—as so many things become clear to them. Jesus' triumphal entry is connected with Lazarus's resurrection. This holds tightly together Jesus' power over death signified by Lazarus's resurrection, and Jesus' own death and coming resurrection which will defeat death forever. Those who saw the sign at Lazarus's tomb will become witnesses to Jesus (and not witnesses of their own beliefs), passing on the good news to the other pilgrims coming to worship God (verse 18). The Pharisees (probably only a small segment) continue to search for the right circumstances to arrest Jesus for mockery of their religion and blasphemy of their God.

Greek Interest in Jesus (12:20-26)

This story has an important theological place for John's Gospel. Apparently some Greeks *who went up to worship* at the feast are in Jerusalem during the Passover. Perhaps they come just to meet Jesus. The term *Greek* implies Hellenists or Gentiles who speak Greek. They probably ask Philip for an introduction because he has a Greek name. He is from a Greek-speaking region of Galilee (Bethsaida), and therefore probably speaks Greek.

Their question to Philip is an important question. They want to *see* Jesus, probably meaning that they want to visit with Jesus. In John's understanding, this could mean that they really want to believe in Jesus. So they ask if Philip could help them in this matter. These Greek-speaking individuals broadly represent the Gentile community, the *other sheep*, that are not of this fold (10:16). We never learn whether they are successful in seeing Jesus. In any case, this theme of universal salvation is evident at many places throughout John's Gospel—especially in Jesus' conversation with

Nicodemus (2:23–3:21), with the woman at the well (chapter 4), and the teachings about sheep (chapter 10).

Philip recruits Andrew and they go to speak with Jesus (verse 22). Jesus gives some general teachings concerning their request. The general theme of these teachings is an explanation of his life and its meaning for his followers. First he explains that his *hour* has come. The *Son of Man* will be glorified. He is about to suffer, die, and be buried. But in the Resurrection/ascension he will glorify God, be glorified himself, and bring glory to humanity standing before God.

Jesus' second teaching begins with the phrase, *Amen, amen* (or, *I guarantee you*). He refers to a grain of wheat dying and bearing fruit (verse 24). A similar use of seed or grain is found in Matthew 13:24-30 and Luke 8:4-8. In each case, the theme has to do with the gift of faith concerning Christ, the seed, and the acceptance of the seed by humanity.

Third, Jesus speaks of putting God first in one's life. Because God freely chooses humanity for fellowship (as noted in the previous verse), God is to become the beginning of life. This important teaching is found in other Gospels (Matthew 6:24; Luke 14:26) as well as the Old Testament (Deuteronomy 5:6-8). To live solely for the Father is to *hate* life independent of the Father. This does not imply that life cannot be enjoyed to its fullest; on the contrary, it must be enjoyed to its fullest. Conversely, to love this life is to disregard living for God. Thus believers are to serve, or give honor, to Christ. And as we give honor, we will be honored as well.

Final Public Teachings (12:27-50)

These are Jesus' final teachings to the crowds (verse 29). At the end of these teachings, Jesus turns to instructing his disciples and acting out the meaning of the new Passover. The teachings follow the normal pattern of John: Events are followed by explanatory teachings or narratives. These teachings are meant to explain the three stories they follow (12:1-26).

In the first section, Jesus openly struggles with his imminent death. This is a public wrestling with the same issues evident at Gethsemane (Mark 14:32-42). After encouraging his followers to be brave and to die for his sake, he now struggles with his own death. He cannot pray for relief from this hour, because it is for this task that he has come.

Then Jesus makes the simple statement that the Father will *glorify his name* (verse 28). God speaks a Word to humanity, and that Word takes the form of action. The Word becomes flesh. Now the reverse happens. Jesus responds by speaking words of glory to the Father and suddenly the words become action. *The glory has come and will come again!* (See Matthew 6:9.)

The crowd thinks they heard thunder, which in the Old Testament can be identified with the voice of God (1 Samuel 12:18; see also Acts 9:7 and 22:9). Others think that they overheard an angel speak to Jesus.

Jesus immediately points out that what happened was for their benefit (verse 30). Jesus as the *Word of God* is God's spoken and acted word to humanity. The judgment of the world is through Christ, and continued eternally through Christ. This continued action and reaction is the heart of the Gospel as a living relationship.

The crowd senses the eternal meaning of what he says (verse 34). This statement may be based on numerous Old Testament records, such as Psalm 89 (especially verse 36).

Jesus answers their question about the Son of man with a saying about light. This is a theme evident from the beginning of John's Gospel. Jesus is the light who shines in the midst of humanity. But soon this light will return to God. In this sense, if we walk in the light, we are walking with God. The darkness is the rebellious world that has turned from God and does not know where it is going. All humanity is made to *walk*, or live, *in the light*. By living in the light, belief is strengthened and one becomes, over a period of time, a child of God.

Now Jesus retreats from the crowds. The Jewish nation has refused to believe in Jesus, though he has done many signs. The Gospel writer now gives us a commentary on why this has happened. The issue remained somewhat of a mystery in the early church (see Romans 9–11, for example). Why did Israel remain so blind to God's truth spoken in Christ, the Word? To explain this, the early church searched their only scriptural source—the Old Testament—and found some understanding in the prophet Isaiah. These words in Isaiah are from an older tradition found in the Torah.

This turning away by Israel is an example of human rebellion against the truth of God. It is an understanding based on God's plan of salvation for all humanity. God's plan demands our worship. But humanity wants to work its own plan. Israel is the perfect example of such independence and rebellion. In this sense, they are the perfect covenant people—and they will always be the primary covenant people.

Isaiah spoke these words because he saw the glory of God (verse 41). He saw God's plan. He had a vision of God's truth. He foresaw the eyes of the Israelites blinded by God's light. Some, of course, did see. But they refused to go against the status quo. They refused to seek God, and chose human acceptance instead. They refused to see God's salvation plan for fear of peer rejection (1 Corinthians 1:22-25). They chose instead to worship human religious activity.

In the final section (verses 44-50), John records some general teachings by Jesus. The themes of these teachings are not new to this Gospel. They include such topics as belief, being sent, light, and darkness. They serve as a fitting theological summary to Jesus' public ministry.

Jesus begins by placing all emphasis on God. He

passes the source of truth through himself and centers its origin and basis in God. Everything emanates from God to humanity. And if we want to see God, the one and only place where we can do that is in the person and work of Christ. When the Christ ascends to the Father, people no longer see Christ directly. We will see him and hear him through the living (in the Spirit) gospel message. In this way, Jesus is the light that identifies and opens the path to the Father. He is the light of the world (see 1 John 1:5-7).

Jesus makes an incredible statement in verse 47. The task given to Jesus by the Father is not to reject and judge. His only work or labor is to save the world, reconcile the world to the Father. Then how are we to be judged? By the *word that I have spoken* (verse 48). If we reject or refuse to receive Jesus' teachings (which are primarily about the Father and himself), then judgment will come.

This does not imply a formal judgment, but a judgment that is natural, correct, and right. Jesus is that Word, and by God's speaking to us, as the Word of the Father, we cannot ignore it. We have been addressed! We have been spoken to! We have been beckoned by God! We cannot ignore God's speech to us.

All that Christ has spoken to us is from God. Again he places all the emphasis on God.

The message is *eternal life* (verse 50). God's *commandment*, or words of life, had strong Jewish significance (Deuteronomy 8:3; 32:46-47). Commandment carries two important understandings: (1) The real command is God's command of salvation fellowship with humanity. This is the command to *eternal life*. (2) This command is finished in Christ. We do not have to rely upon our own strength and righteousness. Christ is bidden by the Father to complete the work of salvation on our behalf. God's Word and act are the same (1:1-5).

§ § § § § § §

The Message of John 11:55–12:50

The opening three stories theologically set the stage for what is coming. First Jesus is anointed following Lazarus's resurrection, and prior to his own burial and resurrection. Second, entering Jerusalem, he is hailed as king of Israel. He is "crowned" as the messianic representative who will defeat death on behalf of his sheep.

Finally, the Greeks, or Gentiles (that is, all humanity) come to him, signaling that his *hour has come*. As God confirmed Jesus at his baptism (Mark 1:11), so now the Father confirms the Son. Jesus is ready to act out his title as the lamb of the Passover festival, the one lamb sacrificed for many. The Jewish community will not accept Jesus, and they finally reject him.

§ § § § § § §

John 13

Introduction to This Chapter

Prior to acting out a new Passover by his actual death and resurrection, Jesus instructs the disciples. He wants to prepare them very carefully for his imminent departure—a departure they do not understand. The writer of John's Gospel tells of two general themes that Jesus emphasizes to his disciples. One has to do with Jesus' work being finished. When he goes to the Father, he will have accomplished the work given him to do. The other theme is that although he will be away, the Holy Spirit will unite them with him and the Spirit will minister to their needs. These two profound truths will stand during the interim period, the time between Jesus' drawing near and his coming again.

Jesus' public ministry now completed, he concentrates his energies on the disciples. They are given his undivided attention. There appear to be no outsiders present as he begins to prepare them for his absence. In his preparation of the disciples, he gives them an important example to follow, an example that summarizes the Gospel's moral meaning.

This chapter has two main parts.

I. The Supper and the Foot Washing (13:1-20)
II. The Betrayal of Judas (13:21-38)

The Supper and the Foot Washing (13:1-20)

This section begins by restating that his *hour* has come. The hour is now identified with the Passover feast. His hour is when he gives new content and meaning to the Passover. But soon he will *depart* from *this world to the Father*. In doing this, he loves his followers, the first believers, who remain in the world of rebellion (17:15). These he loves to the end of his earthly work and life. This verse sets the stage for what is to follow.

They are at supper. Theologically, they are sitting at Passover, remembering God's past kindness to Israel. God's future kindness is unclear. The darkness of this world has already entered Judas, causing him to lose his way. But Jesus is confident, because the Father has prepared the Son for the work that he is about to do. Further, Jesus has made the descent down to the world of rebellion and now he is about to complete his journey, returning to the Father. By Christ coming to humanity and returning to the Father, salvation history is complete.

Jesus dramatically rises from supper. He girds himself with a towel, in the exact manner of a servant, or a priest. Taking water (a frequent symbol in John's Gospel), Jesus begins washing the disciples' feet. First of all, the washing carries the Jewish meaning of purification, or cleansing the self for better communion with God. Second, water symbolizes the Holy Spirit. The disciples are about to receive the Spirit. Third, the cleansing of the feet represents Jesus' death on the cross for humanity.

Peter protests by questioning Jesus' action. This protest introduces Jesus' statements as to why he must wash their feet. Although it does not make sense now, it will later. Peter seems to imply that this is too degrading a task for Jesus (the Christ) and protests again. Here we see two levels of conversation so typical of John's Gospel. Jesus interprets the footwashing on the basis of what he is about to do, his "degrading" death for them. They can *have no part* (NIV; NRSV, *share*) in him unless he washes them—by dying for them. Peter then wants a good scrubbing, completely misunderstanding what Jesus is saying. So Jesus substitutes the word *bath* for the word *wash* (verse 10). If Peter is *bathed* in the death and resurrection and ascension of Christ, washing can be of no advantage. Bathing probably carries more theological meaning than washing. At the end of this narrative, there is a reference to the one who was not really bathed in the work of Christ (verse 11).

Similar to the structure of earlier healing accounts, Jesus now explains and interprets his acts. Jesus resumes his position at the table. This act is a metaphor on his life. He left his position with the Father, washed the disciples clean by his death, and then resumed his position beside the Father. From this vantage point, he now asks, *Do you know* (NRSV; NIV, *understand*) *what I have done to you?* Jesus identifies himself as *Teacher and Lord,* combining it with the phrase, *I am* (verse 13).

Now Jesus tells them of the work they are to do while he is gone. They are to follow his example by washing each other's feet. In this manner, they bear witness to him. This is the heart of Christian living. When it is ignored, daily Christian living becomes a sham. Jesus explains that only if believers live and do as he has done will the chain relationship between believers, Jesus, and the Father be sound.

A further reference to Judas is made. Quoting the Hebrew hymnal (Psalm 41:9), he refers to a *traitor* who is close to him. It is interesting that this psalm was understood by Jewish teachers as a reference to Absalom's conspiracy against David (2 Samuel 15). The verse quoted by Jesus was understood as a commentary on Ahithopel. In this context, the psalm explains that Judas turns away from Jesus as Ahithopel turned against David—he plays the same seeming advantage. Jesus tells the disciples that this will happen so they will better understand that he is *I am* (verse 19; see also Isaiah 48:5).

Then Jesus brings the commentary back to his original theme. Verse 20 is similar to verse 16. Jesus begins in the same manner, *Amen, amen.* The theme in verse 16 is greatness in order or authority (that is, humanity, Christ, God). The theme here is receiving or accepting. In each case, the connecting force is the dual strength of relationship and bearing witness. The two go hand in hand. By following his greatness, we serve others as a response to our reconciliation in Christ and our witness to the Father. All this—as Jesus is about to explain—is possible because of the Holy Spirit.

The Betrayal of Judas (13:21-38)

The contrast between Judas and Peter is astonishing. Peter questions Jesus, but in the end is cleansed. Judas does not question Jesus, but apparently his heart is never cleansed. Peter turns to the light in total commitment. Judas lacks total commitment and enters the darkness of the night to do his work.

Judas's betrayal is taken very seriously indeed. Jesus is troubled in spirit, the same way he was troubled as he stood before Lazarus's tomb (11:33). In each case, he stands in the face of rebellion and darkness, the forces of death that flee from the light. *Amen, amen* is again used to set off the coming important statement. One of his followers will *betray* or turn away from him—one who lacks full and total commitment. The disciples are unaware of what he is saying. As they sit in the normal reclining position, probably around a low table with a horseshoe arrangement of cushions, one of the disciples is *next to him*. This is the disciple *whom Jesus loved*, one of six references to this unknown disciple. It is probable that his is an eyewitness's statement, and therefore a possible "signature" for this Gospel. But, as with Peter, there is a clear contrast between the *beloved disciple* and Judas.

Again Simon Peter is the spokesperson for the group. Peter nods, or signals that he wishes to know of whom Jesus speaks. This question is apparently directed to the *beloved disciple* so that he can relay it to Jesus because he is close to him. Jesus responds by giving a *dipped piece of bread* to Judas, perhaps suggesting that Jesus serves the eucharist to Judas prior to the work he is about to do. Then follows the only time John's Gospel uses the word *Satan* (verse 27). Judas is ready to act and Jesus ordains him to do so. In this manner, Jesus accepts his hour and the imminent crowning act of his reconciling work.

The disciples are unaware of what has transpired. This is not surprising, because all along the disciples are not clear about Jesus' identity, work, or fast-approaching death. In fact, some apparently think that Judas is being sent out to get provisions for their stay in Jerusalem during Passover. This would have been normal because shops would not have stayed open for all of Passover weekend. Others identify his exit with the giving of an offering for the poor. This too was a normal custom during Passover. Then we read the evangelist's commentary (verse 30). Judas takes the morsel and immediately goes out, *and it was night*. Judas has chosen the path he wishes to follow, and rushes away from the light into the darkness and death.

Now that Judas has gone, John records his characteristic theological commentary. In the first portion of this commentary (verses 31-35), Jesus talks about glorifying God and the importance of love among his followers. As soon as Judas leaves, Jesus speaks of being glorified now, and God being glorified. Because Jesus has come from the Father, he must return to the Father for the Father to be glorified. Judas's betrayal indicates the final leg of Jesus' journey back to the Father.

The Son's going out and coming back home dramatically displays the love between the Father and the Son. This same love must be the basis of Jesus' followers' lives. Jesus refers to them as *little children* (NRSV; NIV, *my children*), a term of endearment that defines their status before God because Jesus is their older brother (verse 33). Jesus explains that he is with

110

them now, but soon he will go away (back to the Father) and they cannot come. These men have been with Jesus a long time. They have devoted their lives to Jesus. Now Jesus explains that he is going on ahead in this journey, and they must move at a slower pace behind him.

Then Jesus gives them the famous commandment that they *love one another*. This love stems from the love of the Father and the Son. As the Son came from the Father to humanity, he loved humanity because of what he gave up to reconcile them to the Father (Philippians 2:6-7). Jesus' followers must reflect that same love in their everyday living. But this love is not a result of their own strength. This love is not some form of human love—it is the divine love between the Father and the Son and is empowered by the Holy Spirit in the disciples.

In the second section (verses 36-68) Peter's defection is discussed. Peter boldly responds to Jesus' statements about his leaving and says he will do anything for Jesus, even die. Jesus responds with *Amen, amen,* and John documents the fulfillment of this prediction (18:17-18, 25-27). This little exchange stresses the difficulties ahead for Jesus' followers. It will not be easy. Jesus will be with the Father, and, as for Peter, despite our best intentions, temptations will be great. The greatest temptation will be to defect, to go our own way. Even Peter momentarily makes this mistake—before the Resurrection. Other temptations, such as not living the *new commandment,* and not loving one another, will also be very difficult. Jesus is aware of these difficulties and now begins to address them.

§ § § § § §

The Message of John 13

Prior to Jesus' final teachings to the disciples, he acts. He gives them action prior to explanations, a consistent pattern throughout this Gospel.

First of all, Jesus' followers must live out a life of selfless giving and self-sacrifice, just as Jesus is about to do. We can assume that Jesus' act of footwashing made its greatest impression on the disciples after his death and resurrection.

Second, this love for others is not self-based. It is not dependent upon individual moral fiber and strength. It is an example that comes from Christ and it is empowered by God—just as Christ is empowered by the Father. This power is God's love for humanity through Christ. This godly love is about to be redefined as a work of the Holy Spirit in the disciples.

§ § § § § § §

John 14–15

Introduction to These Chapters

These chapters can be divided into two general themes.
I. Fellowship with the Disciples (14:1-31)
II. The church with the Father (15:1-27)

Fellowship with the Disciples (14:1-31)

Jesus begins by contrasting the disciples' troubles with
his own troubles. Do not be *troubled*, he says to them.
Because I am troubled for you, you need not be troubled.
Instead, trust in the Father and in me. Jesus speaks of the
reconciling work he is about to complete. Because of this
imminent death experience for humanity, he is troubled.
But he is their assurance; because he is troubled, their
hearts should be calm—they should trust in him.

Then Jesus directs their attention to the good things
that will happen because he goes away. Jesus' reference
to his *Father's house* may carry two meanings. Following
the interpretation of the early church father Origen (A.D.
185–255), Jesus could be referring to many resting places
along the Christian journey of faith. Thus persons would
move from room to room, depending upon the length,
duration, and speed of their spiritual journey. Or *house*
could refer to a final dwelling place after this life is
completed (traditionally heaven). In either case, the
believer dwells with the Father *through and in* the Son.

Now the Son must go and *prepare,* or by his death
make available, the Father's house with many rooms. He

will return to fetch them. Based on the interpretation of *house*, Jesus is saying that he will continually give them rooms as they journey in faith and he will be there to meet them when their journey is over. *And you* (they) *know the way (I am* the way) *to the place where I am going* (to the Father) (verse 4). Jesus is the only way to the Father.

But Thomas has a question. Jesus' last statement is not clear, and he previously had not answered Peter. Part of Thomas's question *(How can we know the way?)* suggests that humanity cannot know the way, except it be given from God (1:33). Jesus' answer to Thomas summarizes what he has been teaching them. The three terms, *the way, the truth, and the life,* explain Jesus as the door to the sheepfold. He is the way to the Father, the truth about the Father, and the life with the Father.

By seeing and knowing Jesus, we know the Father. There is no deception here, only truth; there are not many paths, only one; there are not many lives, only one life with the Father. And all this is true because humanity is freely chosen by God through Christ. Thus *Christ is all and in all* (Colossians 3:11). There is nothing else!

It is interesting that "doubting" Thomas asks the question here. Undoubtedly there is tremendous temptation to add to the person of Christ, to help him help his followers. Thomas betrays a sense of not trusting, or doubting that Jesus is the *only* way, truth, and life. This kind of doubt remains a great temptation for humanity.

Now Philip carries on the conversation. Representing many believers through the centuries, he wants more visual proof before he will be satisfied. Jesus' response is to the point, reiterating that he is the way, truth, and life. Human friendship fosters trust. Jesus speaks here of a friendship or relationship between himself and his followers that goes far beyond human friendship. Because he and the Father are one (verse 7), friendship with Christ is a relationship with the Father. Jesus wonders how Philip can ask such a question.

Then Jesus explains that he and the Father are *in* each other, meaning deep communion and fellowship (verse 10). This deep fellowship is signified by intense communications of words and works between the Father and the Son. Jesus is already understood as the Word of God spoken and acted toward humanity. If this is too great a mystery, then believe, as you did with Moses, the signs that I do.

Now that the rock of the faith is clarified, Jesus explains their relationship to the rock. He begins this powerful section with the strong words, *Truly, truly*. Because Jesus did great works during his days on earth, his followers will do great things because of him. His followers will not do works by their own strength, but by the strength of Christ. This will happen because he goes *to the Father*. As he stands before the Father, representing all humanity, miraculous things are possible—but only in accord with the Father's will (verse 13; see also Matthew 6:10).

Thus as Jesus represents humanity before the Father, prayerful asking is commanded and demanded from his followers. Whatever is asked in the *name of the Son* and brings glory to the Father will be done. What a powerful promise to the children of the Father! But the conditions of such a promise must not be overlooked.

Is this type of prayer merely self-help? How do we really pray? By our own strength? No, there is far greater help for the disciples of Jesus. They are not left to their own resources. Jesus explains that if we love him and keep his commandments, he will pray, or request that the Father give his followers another *Counselor* (NIV; NRSV, *Advocate*), the *Spirit of truth*. This Holy Spirit will replace Jesus' presence with them. Or better, it will make Jesus' absence into his presence with them! Like Jesus, God's Spirit will counsel them and keep them close to Jesus forever. And not anyone can receive this Spirit. Only those who follow Jesus, who go through the one door, who follow the way, truth, and life—only they can fully receive this Spirit. The Spirit is sent—because of Jesus' prayer and work and life—to those who follow him.

The Spirit will not allow Jesus' disciples to be *desolate* or abandoned (verse 18). Jesus will come to them through and in the Spirit. As a result, they will see Jesus, that is, see him because of their living relationship with him through the Spirit. The world cannot do this, because it does not have the Spirit available through Christ's reconciling work. The Spirit will confirm and make known the relationship between the Father and the Son, and between the Son and his disciples. This deep love relationship is reflected in the keeping of the love commandments.

Judas then asks an important question. How will Christ be present to them and not the world? Jesus' answer assumes his mighty work. As the Father loves the Son and the Son the Father, the Son does the work of the Father. So also with his disciples. As the Father loves the Son and therefore the disciples of the Son, the disciples will seek only the work of the Father. They will commune together in a constant and living love relationship. In this manner, the disciples will be in right relationship with the Father through the Son. The world of rebellion, which rejects this relationship, will not know the Father through the Son.

Jesus concludes this section by speaking again about the Holy Spirit. He has spoken to them but they will not fully understand just now. The counselor will come because of Christ, and will help them recall and understand what he is saying. How could they have understood what he was saying with the Resurrection and ascension yet to come? How could they follow his explanation yet? Now he is with them; soon the Spirit will come to replace his absence, for he must go to the Father on their behalf. Thus he gives them *peace,* salvation with the Father through him.

116

After repeating the opening statement, Jesus explains that if they love him they will rejoice because he is going away. Of course they do not understand—but they will. Their gift of love will deepen through the teaching and guidance of the Holy Spirit. Soon they will understand that the Father is greater in that God's plan of salvation for humanity is being wrought in Christ. This will glorify the Father. Jesus' time now grows short; he must begin his homeward journey to the Father.

The Church with the Father (15:1-27)

Jesus begins this section with the statement *I am*. The next several verses offer a wonderful description of the church, the body of Christ. Jesus is the *vine* and the Father tills or prepares the soil. The branches are the disciples who depend upon the vine that is cultivated by the Father. This is another way of saying theologically what Jesus had previously taught, that the Father's plan of salvation is for the Son to journey into the soil, reconciling and uniting the vinedresser with the branches. The end result of this loving, caring relationship is the bearing of more fruit, that is, witnessing to the Son and to the Father. The Father is careful to prune, literally to clean, the branches—in Christ. The emphasis of pruning is not on the negative side of disciplining and reprimanding, or cutting back, but more on the positive side of putting a branch right with the purpose of the vinedresser—with God's great plan of salvation. The dead branches, those out of relationship with the vine, are simply taken away.

This description reminds us of the *tree of life* in the Garden of Eden (Genesis 2:9). This tree has represented ongoing life and eternal life in many Semitic religions. At the center of Jewish worship is a seven-candlestick lampstand (the menorah) which represents the tree of life (Exodus 25:31-37). In the book of Revelation, the tree of life is an important image (Revelation 2:7; 22:2).

This theme is developed in the verses that follow. Jesus is the *Word* spoken to us and we are clean before the Father through him. Branches must remain on the vine; the disciples must remain in a living relationship with Christ. This alone will please the vinedresser.

The first four verses concentrate on the relation between the Father and the Son. The branches have a place because of the vine and vinedresser. Now, Jesus can speak more emphatically of the branches. An abiding relationship with Christ bears fruit; an unliving relationship leads to darkness, death, and destruction.

What form does this *abiding* take? The form is conversation or prayer. As long as we abide, we can, should, and must ask for things. This glorifies the Father, because much fruit is produced. It is important to notice that "abiding" and "producing fruit" are the basis of prayer. If we abide, our prayers will be in accordance with God's will—a will that is made clear to us through continual abiding. So our prayers are for God's will, not our will. They are meant to produce fruit for the Father, not for ourselves.

This abiding is another word for love (verse 9). The love that bonds the Son to the Father is the love that bonds the disciples to Jesus. The result is keeping the commandment (of love) as the disciples journey through this world—much like the Son has kept the commandment or work of the Father in reconciling humanity. This alone brings joy. If humanity is made for fellowship with the Father, this fellowship alone brings completion or peace. The full joy of the Son is doing the will of the Father. And the Father joys in the Son, fulfilling his will. Thus there are two joys Jesus' followers can know: the joy of being reconciled to the Father and the joy of doing the Father's will. Both of these will make the disciples' joy *complete*.

Jesus' followers will be known by their life of *love* (verse 12). Their lives will reflect God's love for humanity expressed through Christ. This life of love among Jesus' followers is a lifelong calling—a true vocation. The best example of this love characteristic is Jesus' self-sacrifice.

Friendship with Jesus constitutes the source of love. The new designation of Jesus' followers is not servant or slave. They are not forced to do good things and love others by their own strength. Their strength comes from the Father's love of the Son and the Son's love and self-sacrifice for humanity. This makes Jesus' disciples much more than servants; this makes them *children*, or friends of the Father.

God first comes to us. God first chooses us. Not only did God freely choose to have fellowship with us, but because humanity is reconciled in Christ, we are now *appointed*. Because of Christ's self-sacrifice, we are appointed to bear fruit. The harvest of fruit is not meant to abide in the disciples, but the newly harvested fruit is meant to abide through Christ the vine with the vinedresser. If we accept this appointment as our lifelong vocation, then *ask the Father in my name* and it will be done. How could anyone miss with this foundation of prayer? Jesus ends by commanding them to live out their appointments to vocation.

This life of love and self-sacrifice will bring persecution. The world will hate this attitude and lifestyle because it promotes values different from those of the world. The world cannot stand this difference. That is why the world has not accepted Jesus. And because Jesus chose these disciples, the world will not easily accept them—the implication is that the world will never accept them. To show this more clearly, Jesus uses his previous instruction about sending forth (13:16), receiving (13:20), knowing (14:7), living (14:19), and loving (14:23). The same holds true with regard to persecution. Because God's plan of salvation is rejected by humanity, Christ is persecuted. Jesus' followers will experience the same—although some will respond to their words of spoken and acted testimony. All this will happen because they do not know God and do not wish to know God. They prefer to remain rebellious (verse 21; see also 1 Samuel 22:22; Jeremiah 14:21).

Because Christ came and spoke explicitly and directly to all, humanity must now respond. Refusal to hear the Son and accept his work is refusal to hear the Father. Jesus concludes by quoting Psalm 35:19.

Maintaining the abiding relationship between vinedresser, vine, and branches, Jesus emphasizes again the coming Holy Spirit (verses 26-27). Now Jesus will send the Counselor after he has gone to the Father. Before he promised to pray that the Father send the Counselor (14:16). But in the face of the coming persecutions and rejections, the *Spirit of truth* will come and unite the unaware disciples with the Son.

§ § § § § § §

The Message of John 14–15

Chapter 14 records Jesus' teachings about his relationship with the disciples after he is glorified. Chapter 15 discusses how believers are to live daily while Jesus is away with the Father. Taken together, these two chapters offer a firsthand account of what Jesus wanted his followers to know just prior to his departure.

Before Christ, the law was a guide for responding to God's love expressed toward Israel. Now Christ is about to accomplish all for humanity. We cannot use the law and respond to God. But Christ's work will be complete and he will soon be present before the Father on our behalf. Already there is no escaping the Father's address or word spoken to humanity in Christ.

§ § § § § § §

John 16–17

Introduction to These Chapters

In chapter 15, Jesus explained to his disciples that they would be hated as Jesus' followers. Now he becomes more explicit as he teaches how this will happen. The outline is as follows.

    I. Jesus' Followers in the World (16:1-33)

    II. Jesus' Prayer for His Followers (17:1-26)

Jesus' Followers in the World (16:1-33)

Jesus' overriding concern is that the disciples be kept from falling away (verse 1), or be kept from being shaken loose from their relationship with him. He knows that they can lose their way, be lured into the darkness, and become a dead branch. This will happen especially in the synagogues, where people will reject the followers of Jesus the Messiah. They will even murder the disciples, thinking that they will be blessed by God for such good work (verse 2). Paul is a good example of this (Acts 8:1-3; 26:9; Galatians 1:13-14). The reason for such thinking is that they are in the darkness. Jesus' prophetic statements are meant to give meaning and understanding to these future persecutions, perhaps making them easier to bear.

Jesus now shows great sensitivity to the disciples' reception of his teachings. They are troubled, and he is aware of it. He had not told them about the persecutions because he was with them, and he was the one being persecuted. But now his hour has come; it is time for him to return to the Father. The disciples have heard his disturbing statements and are literally saddened—not just by his going away, but also because the road ahead will be very difficult. But only if Jesus goes will two things happen, both to their advantage: He will fully reconcile humanity before and with the Father, and he will send the Counselor to help him.

The Counselor will have a great and important role. It will not be the disciples' teachings and witness that will direct people to the Father via the Son; this will be the work of the Holy Spirit. Sin and belief, righteousness in relation to the Father, judgment and darkness, all are made known only by the Holy Spirit. The disciples are called to bear witness. They will be persecuted for their witness. This is their thankful response to God for the salvation of humanity. But the work of salvation is God's, and not the work of humanity. Here Jesus explains that it is the Holy Spirit who unites branches with the vine and the vinedresser. The disciples may be saddened because of persecution, but the work of salvation will never be their responsibility or burden.

Along with persecution comes the excitement of understanding and insight (verses 12-15). Jesus implies that he will tell them many more things, but not now. These new things will come through the living relationship that will continue between the disciples and Jesus when he is with the Father. The implication is that he will always speak to them—and they should listen! The link that binds the disciples to the soon-to-ascend Christ is the Spirit of truth. He will relay messages constantly and so *glorify* the Son and the Father.

In the next section Jesus again tells the disciples about his going away. This time he adds a statement about his returning. It is not surprising that the disciples are even more confused, and begin to mumble among themselves (like Israel of old). They ask him to explain the phrase *a little while* (verse 18). This was a sensitive issue in the early church, and it is not surprising that it is singled out in the last Gospel written. Perhaps its readers and writers wished an explanation as to why *a little while* meant such a long delay in Jesus' return. And perhaps John recalled Jesus speaking about just this issue. Jesus repeats their question, further indicating what a vital question this was for first-century Christians.

Jesus begins his explanation and answer to their question with the emphatic phrase, *Amen, amen.* First using a general statement of contrasts, he explains how the disciples will be persecuted because of their witness, and the world will be delighted. This will happen while he is away. But because he will return, their temporary and interim sorrow will turn to real joy. To explain this further, Jesus uses the example of a woman in childbirth. The implication is that as the disciples bear witness to him, the Spirit will be blessing their testimony and God's plan of salvation will be complete. The Kingdom will be born—but only with suffering and strain. After the child is delivered, the pain is not only replaced by joy but it is forgotten. They will be sorrowful now, but Christ will see them again, either when they die or when he returns. Then their joy will be complete.

When Christ does return, they will not ask him any questions because everything will be clear. Their abiding relationship, while he was away, will then be complete (1 Corinthians 13:12). But in the meantime, during the interim period, Jesus tells them to make requests *in my name* to the Father. Their vocation is to be his witness; ask accordingly. They have yet to ask because Christ has not yet risen and ascended to the Father. But this will soon take place. So ask while I'm away, Jesus says, and your joy will be full—not complete; it will be complete when I return. But now it can be full, so ask in my name.

Jesus then explains why they are having such a hard time understanding what he is saying. He is speaking in figures, in parables, and he is speaking about the future.

They will change when he is away with the Father and sends the Spirit. His work must be completed before his teaching makes sense and all this works itself out. Then they will understand the Father more clearly (through him) and they can ask in his name. He will not have to pray on their behalf for acceptance and reconciliation with the Father. The Father already loves them because of the Son. That is why he sent the Son, and they are soon to be fully reconciled with the Father through the life of the Son. Christ's dual movements of descending and now imminent ascending to the Father are restated. This is the full work of reconciliation.

This section ends with the disciples saying what they in fact do not understand. They summarize Jesus' teachings as a confession. This is probably an admission by the Gospel writer that though the disciples could say the words, they had yet to live their meaning, and this is precisely what they were called and commissioned to do: Live their meaning. Jesus' answer predicts their desertion and ends with the phrase, *I am* never alone. The inner fellowship of the Godhead (Father, Son, and Holy Spirit) is the essence of life. It is this fellowship that spills over, creating humanity and now reconciling humanity for fellowship with the Godhead.

Jesus' final magnificent words speak of the disciples' peace. This peace comes through abiding fellowship with the Father through the Son and in the Spirit. It is just this living relationship with God that will cause trials and tribulations in the world. This will all happen during the interim period, during the time Jesus is away with the Father. But the disciples are not to worry. With Jesus' return to the Father, the world will be defeated or overcome. As long as the disciples stay close and abide in the Son with the Father (through the Spirit), they will have peace—not because of human spirituality, but because of Christ's victorious return to the Father and sending of the Spirit.

Jesus' Prayer for His Followers (17:1-26)

After Jesus' instruction to the disciples, he now offers a prayer. This prayer is a prayer without equal. It is the summation of what Jesus had done, is doing, and will do. Here is the summary of his reconciling work. The three parts of the prayer are vaguely aligned to the three chapters of discourse Jesus spoke to the disciples. Section one of the prayer deals with Jesus' work and mission to the Father (verses 1-5); section two records Jesus' concern for the disciples (verses 6-19); and section three is comprised of petitions for future believers (verses 20-26).

Part of the uniqueness of this chapter in John's Gospel is its relation to a similar situation in the other Gospels. In them, this prayer is prayed in the Garden of Gethsemane (Matthew 26:36-46; Mark 14:32-42; Luke 22:40-46). The prayer's presentation in the other Gospels is very important. The other Gospels emphasize the setting of the prayer; John's Gospel emphasizes the content of the prayer. Hence both are necessary for a proper understanding of this event.

In the synoptics, Jesus takes his disciples to the *garden* (similar in meaning to *Eden*). He tells them to *sit here* (Mark 14:32) while he goes ahead to pray. He takes Peter, James, and John a little farther; then, greatly troubled, he tells them to wait and watch while he goes ahead and prays. In order to pray for them, he withdraws from them (as he soon will do by dying). But they tend to fall asleep, not praying and not waiting for his return. He says to Peter, *Are you asleep? Could you not keep watch for one hour? Watch and pray so that you will not fall into temptation. The spirit is willing, but the body is weak* (Mark 14:37-38 NIV). This same thing happens again (see Mark 14:40). Later, Peter and the others abandon Jesus when he is arrested in the same Garden of Gethsemane.

If Jesus had not come to the disciples *in his prayer* or prayed for them, the disciples would have slept through the night. The disciples (or the church) denied Jesus.

They did not participate in his reconciling work. They left him alone. He acted alone—for them. In the synoptic Gospels, we find a much more severe picture of Jesus praying for the church and disciples prior to his arrest and crucifixion. Here we see more clearly the believers' non-participation in God's act of reconciliation through Christ for humanity. The disciples offer no corresponding act to the work of Christ. He alone watches and prays for the disciples, for the church, for all believers. Hence Jesus tells Peter, the disciple we can accept as representative of Jesus' followers: *Simon, Simon, listen! Satan has demanded to sift all of you like wheat, but I have prayed for you that your own faith may not fail . . .* (Luke 22:31-32 NRSV).

On the one hand and from the side of humanity, the flesh is very weak. The *flesh* must be taken very seriously. With the bridegroom in their midst (3:29), with God having drawn so near in Christ, they still cannot keep awake. They still cannot make a contribution to the work Christ is about to complete. Their flesh gets in the way. They cannot watch or pray. Their eyes are heavy. They can do nothing else but sleep. (See Paul's statements in Romans 7; 2 Corinthians 12:9-10.)

On the other hand and from God's side, how great is the work of Christ! Jesus goes before humanity reconciling the world to the Father. His life is our prayer. Humanity has nothing else—no other prayer. But in his life of word and act, reconciliation is complete. It is also worth mentioning that the New Testament book of Hebrews offers an excellent background to this chapter of John's Gospel.

Jesus' Mission with the Father (17:1-5)

The first section of the prayer deals with Jesus' relation to the Father. Jesus addresses God with the intimate term *Father*. The Father is the subject of the prayer, the one to whom everything is directed.

Jesus' hour has come. It is time for him to finish the work he has been sent to do and go through the final intense moments of conflict between light and darkness, heaven and hell, life and death. This hour begins the Son's glorification. Glory comes during the work of reconciliation, in that the Father sustains and supports the Son. Glory also comes with the completion of the work. In the same manner, the Father sustains and glorifies the disciples during their lives and at the completion of their lives.

Jesus has *power over all flesh* (i.e., *people;* verse 2). He alone prays and watches for humanity. He alone lives a life that properly responds to God's gracious and free choosing of humanity for fellowship. He alone leads the way to the Father as a forerunner for humanity (Hebrews 6:20). The work of reconciliation that he alone accomplishes for us gives him power over flesh and the bestowing of eternal life or eternal fellowship with the Father. The Father is glorified or worshiped by the completed work of reconciliation. This completed work unites the Father and humanity in peace.

The concluding statement of the opening lines summarizes Jesus' descending to earth and ascending back to the Father. Verse 5 reminds us of the opening lines of John. The Son is sent on a mission to lead humanity to the Father. He will soon be back in the Father's presence, as he was *before the world* was created. This mission and work were not without pain, suffering, and effort on the part of God—hence the references to glory. But soon the circle will be completed; Jesus will be back in the direct presence of the Father as he was before Creation.

Jesus' Concern for His Disciples (17:6-19)

The second portion of the prayer (verses 6-19) is the largest section. The content of these verses centers on the disciples. Jesus is concerned for them. Now that he is about to return to the Father, we get the impression that he is already there, praying and communing with the Father on behalf of the unassuming disciples. This is a foretaste of what he is about to do.

Jesus begins by stating how he has manifested, or revealed, the name of God to them. All thinking about God begins with God. Humanity is not meant to invent God—although that is characteristic of the darkness.

Jesus manifests the Father to the disciples he is given. The Father has guided the Son in choosing the disciples, and they know that the Father and the Son are one. Also, Jesus seems to be saying that during the events of this final hour, the disciples' knowledge will reach greater fullness.

Jesus uses the important phrase *I am* when he states that he is praying for the disciples. He is praying for the disciples, and not the world, because, for all intents and purposes, the disciples are already reconciled to the Father. The hour has begun and they are in the midst of this hour. Even though they finally abandon ship at the height of the storm, they will be rescued. They have been chosen to carry on a work of witness. Their reconciliation is with the Father through Christ, and only through Christ with the Father.

Jesus has begun his homeward journey from the far country. Because his destination is set and he is on course, he is really no longer of this world. But the disciples must remain. Jesus is concerned for their well-being. He is concerned that they not fall asleep and that they be kept in an abiding relationship with the Father through the Son and in the Spirit. The *oneness* in verse 11 could be understood in a secondary sense as a reference to the unity of the church. But the primary reference and context of this section is to oneness as a right relationship with the Father through the Son.

When Jesus was near them, he kept them. As God drew near in Christ, God's power held them close to the

Father. Jesus has guarded them, protected them, and watched over them. Only one was lost, Judas, who ran away from the light into the darkness. But soon Jesus will be absent from them and with the Father. They will have the Counselor that Jesus will send—the Holy Spirit or Spirit of truth. The Counselor will unite them with the Father through the Son and make their joy full. Jesus' concern for the disciples is that because they will be hated they must cling to the Father's Word, that is, Christ. Jesus prays that they be kept strong (Matthew 6:13) in order to resist the *evil one* (1 John 2:13-14), or that they not *fall asleep* (Matthew 25:1-13).

Jesus concludes by praying that they be *sanctified* or made holy *by the truth* (verse 17). The truth is the Word, and the Word is Jesus Christ. The Word reconciles them to the Father and makes them holy. Now they can be sent into the world as witnesses to Christ. So Christ is *consecrated* or made holy. He will finish his work and live out a perfect life of worship to the Father. Upon his return to the Father, he will have consecrated his humanity, and therefore all humanity, so that the disciples may be established in the truth of God's holy Word.

Prayers for Future Believers (17:20-26)

In the last section, Jesus prays for future believers. Because of the disciples' witness to the Christ, others will follow. Jesus understands the unity of the Father and the Son as a model for the unity of believers with them and therefore the unity of believers among themselves. The glory of the Son and the Father refer to his finished work of reconciliation, his returning to the Father with our perfect humanity. The oneness of the followers with the Father through the Son will then become a witness to the world.

The future of those who believe and bear witness is eternal. They will be in right relation with the Son and therefore with the Father; they will behold his glory from before the world; and they will live and share in the divine love between the Father and the Son. Jesus' *knowing* of the Father means being in perfect relationship. He has already made his truth known to his disciples; he will continue to make it known until his return. This is the love that freely flows from the Father through the Son to humanity.

§ § § § § § §

The Message of John 16–17

Jesus prepared the disciples for his departure in a threefold manner. First, he gave them an example when he washed their feet. Then he taught them and counseled them. And now, finally, he prays for them.

Jesus' entire life is a prayer on behalf of humanity. In a very real way, the words of this prayer are literally the acts of his life. With Christ praying for humanity with a life so lived, and now presented before the Father for eternity, how could Jesus' followers not pray during this interim period while he is away? How could anyone trivialize his sacrificial work by not praying?

In chapter 17 we overhear Jesus praying *in the earthly temple* of his flesh, just as the Israelites prayed in the earthly Temple in Jerusalem. But now Christ prays in the *heavenly temple* before the very throne of God. He prays for all those who accept through the gift of faith his completed work of reconciliation.

§ § § § § § §

John 18–19

Introduction to These Chapters

Other than Jesus sending the disciples forth, these are the final events of Jesus' life. In the next three chapters, Jesus lives out the new meaning and content of Passover. He now becomes the history of Passover. Previously, John recorded the explanation and rationale of the new Passover. Now it becomes a reality in three parts: the arrest and trial of Jesus (18:1–19:16); the death and burial of Jesus (19:17-42); and the resurrection of Jesus (20:1-31). These sections contain two major themes: God's judgment of human rebellion spoken in Christ's arrest, crucifixion, and burial; and God's grace expressed in the Resurrection.

The events surrounding Jesus' sufferings speak loudly to humanity. They are not accounts for subjective empathizing and opportunities for experiencing human remorse.

Here again Jesus goes before us, as he did in prayer in the previous chapter. But here he goes before us living out a perfect life of worship to the Father. He is always in control of his life. In this sense, he is the true representative of humanity who takes our place and suffers all the consequences of rebellion. He alone stands before the judge of the universe. He suffers all this. And God speaks loudly and clearly: "No! I cannot accept your rebellion!"

John 18–19 may be outlined as follows.

    I. The Arrest (18:1-11)

The Arrest (18:1-11)

Jesus is in charge of the situation; this fact is implied in the first verse. He leads his disciples across the Kidron Valley to a garden. Symbolically, this could be interpreted in many ways. It could be understood as God leading the remnant Israel across the Jordan to the Promised Land. It could be explained in relation to the first Adam analogy (Romans 5:12-21) and the Garden of Eden (Genesis 2–3). It could be related to David's flight from Absalom (2 Samuel 15:23) into the wilderness. Finally, the priest Shimei is *struck down* for crossing the Kidron in order to retrieve slaves (1 Kings 2:36-46). After they cross the Kidron, which separates Jerusalem and the Mount of Olives, they enter the garden together.

Immediately Judas is mentioned. Judas is not with them; he has gone out and has apparently been absent for Jesus' final teachings. He becomes an evil intrusion into the garden. Jesus, we are told, often met with his disciples in this place. This tranquil garden of Gethsemane was perhaps the place for part of his new teachings (14:31). Judas arrives with strong forces. He is accompanied by Roman soldiers and the Temple police, who carry *lanterns, torches* and *weapons*. In John this equipment implies false lights and instruments of rebellion. Judas had previously gone into the night, and he now returns with the instruments of the night.

A dramatic situation unfolds. Jesus asks whom they seek. They answer, *Jesus of Nazareth*, possibly an answer associated with the Nazirites who were dedicated to the will of God. Jesus responds, *I am* the one. Judas and the soldiers of darkness fall to the ground at Jesus' response. They perhaps are momentarily staggered by the phrase *I am*, and Jesus' identity with that phrase (see Psalm 35:4; Isaiah 28:13).

Jesus, fully in control, questions them once again. He relentlessly examines their goal and mission. They give the same response. Jesus repeats his direct answer, adding that the others should be released because he is the one they seek. The disciples represent all humanity. Hence the lamb of God is prepared to go in the place of the many as a ransom for humanity. This is explained in the next verse in reference to Jesus' prayer on behalf of the disciples. The greater meaning is that Jesus' life will be given for them.

Peter attempts to fight back on the basis of his own strength. All the Gospels report this incident. Here we are told that Peter cuts off the ear of Malchus, *the high priest's slave* (NRSV; NIV, *servant*). The symbolism is significant. On the one hand, the incident bears witness to the inability of the Jewish religion (represented by the high priest's slave) to hear and listen to the Word of God (1:14). The Jews do not allow God the freedom to speak once again, following the work of Moses. On the other hand, Peter attempts to use human power to correct the situation. Jesus reprimands him, explaining that his particular work will eternally correct the situation. In this garden, Jesus will drink the cup of his Father and put humanity right with God.

Jesus Is Taken to Caiaphas (18:12-14)

The forces of darkness momentarily *arrest* and *bind* Jesus. He now represents all humanity in the midst of rebellion. They lead him to Annas, who has been high priest. Perhaps he is the authority behind his son-in-law, the high priest Caiaphas. Perhaps he better represents the institution of human-centered religion. After this informal hearing, Jesus is brought before Caiaphas, the one who has given theological justification and explanation for crucifying this troublemaker.

Jesus Is Examined (18:15-27)

Annas's informal examination of Jesus is recorded in verses 15-24. Peter and another disciple follow the crowd that takes Jesus away. The other disciple, who may be the author of this Gospel, *was known* by the high priest. It is not clear if this means friendship or simply visible recognition, but certainly he is allowed to enter the courtyard of Annas's palace. Peter is not allowed to enter immediately until the other disciple speaks for him.

When Peter does enter, a maid asks (expecting a negative answer) if he is a follower of Jesus. His reply is the opposite of Jesus' self-identity: *I am not.* Then in the midst of the darkened courtyard, Peter warms himself by the fire. The courtyard is cold and dark, and the fire provides momentary warmth and light.

Meanwhile, Jesus is questioned. Jesus' reply is that he has attempted to hide nothing; he has not taught in private. There are many witnesses to what he has taught. Rather than giving a summary, he suggests that they ask those who have heard him teach. Jesus is struck on the face, a clear sign of what is to come. Jesus is asked why he is disrespectful to the representative of human religion. Jesus' response is that he speaks the truth from God and therefore not the truth from humanity. If he speaks the truth, why rebel and strike against the truth? Jesus is now sent out, without further questioning. We are not told what happens before Caiaphas. This suggests that Annas is the more important authority.

Now Peter is again questioned. For a second and third time he denies any association with Jesus, using the negative response, *I am not.* Then the ear-cutting in the garden is used to associate Peter with Jesus. Peter had *heard* Jesus; his questioners had not heard Jesus. This third time Peter is questioned in a positive way, expecting an affirmative reply. Again the answer is negative, and the cock crows, suggesting that it is about 3:00-5:00 A.M. Here is the entire spiritual journey of Peter—from negative questions to positive questions. But his reply is still the same. As with all biblical personalities at some point, Peter here reveals his rebellious and dark side.

Jesus in the Praetorium (18:28–19:16)

After a formal hearing before Caiaphas (and probably the Sanhedrin), Jesus is brought to Pilate in the praetorium. *It was early,* suggesting that dawn is approaching. Now that Jesus has been rejected *during the night* by the Jewish leaders, the final stage of his reconciling work for all humanity has begun. At last, it is *daybreak.* The Jews stay back from the praetorium, the Roman official's headquarters, in order to remain pure for Passover. Contact with Gentiles would have made them unclean for the festival (Acts 10:28).

An interesting conversation is now reported. Pilate comes out to them, asking why they have brought Jesus to him. They claim that he is a *criminal,* and Pilate insists that they submit him to their own religious law, which deals with evil deeds having religious overtones. But they want him put to death and they apparently need Roman approval—perhaps because a riot could develop. So Pilate is forced to confront Jesus because of the Jewish negative witness and by their limited conversation.

The conversation between Jesus and Pilate is dramatic indeed. Pilate's question indicates that he is aware of the charges brought against Jesus (verse 3). Jesus answers Pilate's question by questioning Pilate. He asks the source of Pilate's statement. Is it from yourself or the Jews? God is not a possibility here. Pilate's response is, of course, that he is not a Jew. In fact, he personally has no information about Jesus; the Jewish nation has *borne witness* to him—as they will do throughout history. In

typical Johannine style, the conversation moves to two
different levels. Pilate asks what he has done. Jesus'
answer is in terms of kingship and Kingdom, claiming
that his realm *is not of this world* (verse 36). Pilate's
response is that he in fact is claiming to be a king. Jesus
then summarizes his person and work from the Father.
His birth identifies who he is and his work is *to bear
witness to the truth*. He is God and the truth is that God
chooses fellowship with humanity. Pilate's response
directs everything to the person, Jesus: *What is truth?*
(verse 38). Only silence follows. The truth is Jesus.

Pilate's first response is interesting. Although the Jews
saw Pilate as an insensitive official, the followers of Jesus
generally saw him in a more tolerable manner. This was
probably because Jesus was understood to have been put
to death at the promptings of the Jewish leaders. After
all, the Romans were just attempting to keep the peace.
Hence, in the next few verses, Pilate is presented in a
good light. He tells the Jews he finds no fault in Jesus. He
offers them their customary release of a prisoner
(although no such custom has ever been identified with
Passover), and suggests that Jesus, their *King,* be
released. But the crowd asks for Barabbas, a man
described as a robber or bandit. This term describing
Barabbas has been used to speak of a revolutionary or
insurrectionist (Mark 15:7; Luke 23:19). Pilate perhaps
has a deeper motive here—to get rid of the revolutionary!
The Jewish authorities, primarily for religious purposes
and perhaps secondarily for revolutionary purposes,
want Barabbas released.

Things move quickly now. Jesus is given the routine
treatment of scourging. Then the soldiers *mock* him with a
crown, a robe, and an assortment of slaps (see Revelation
17:4; 18:16). Pilate then states his noncommittal attitude
concerning the whole situation. Jesus dramatically appears
before the crowd and Pilate says, *Here is the man* (verse 5).

Here is Jesus in the fullness of his humanity, mockingly crowned and robed.

The immediate response of the Jewish leaders is to crucify him. Pilate again places the burden on the Jewish authorities. Now the truth emerges from their accusations: *He has claimed to be the Son of God.* Pilate seems to be concerned that trouble may come from this—especially if he is just making self-claims. This drives him to again question Jesus. He asks, *Where are you from?* and *Do you not know that I have power?* Jesus' answer stresses Jewish responsibility and places Pilate squarely under the authority of God.

Pilate makes one more attempt to release Jesus. This time he is threatened with lack of patriotism to Caesar. If Jesus claims to be a king, he is a danger to Caesar. Then Jesus is placed in the judgment seat, a dramatic symbol of exactly what he is doing and will soon complete. On the one hand he represents all humanity before God (as the *Son of man*). On the other hand, there he sits on the very pavement of human life, representing all humanity before the powers of this world (as the *Son of God*). It is *noon* (*the sixth hour*) on the preparation day for Passover.

Crucifixion and Death (19:17-37)

Jesus is forced to carry his cross. Much like Isaac, he carries the wood for his own sacrifice (Genesis 22:6). He is taken out to the place of the "skull," an area that perhaps literally resembled a skull. He is crucified with two others. No details are given other than his place between the other two. Here Jesus represents humanity "in the midst of," or between these persons (Isaiah 53:12). Jesus' title as *king* is placed on the cross by Pilate. The title is written in the three common languages of the day, meaning that this is a universal proclamation for all humanity. The seriousness of this proclamation is protested by the Jewish authorities, but Pilate refuses to budge. Ironically, Pilate's insistence and action is prophetic, because it anticipates the coming Gentile acceptance of Christ's kingdom and kingship.

The soldiers then divide Jesus' garments among themselves. These garments strongly symbolize Jesus' priestly office. Thus Jesus is not only a king, but a priest whose hour has come. Using the Old Testament, John accents the detail of the crucifixion. Psalm 22:18 is quoted in verse 24. This particular psalm tells of suffering not unlike a crucifixion. Jesus' garments are aligned with a priest's garments (Exodus 28:4; Leviticus 16:4). His garments are divided by the four soldiers; his coat was without seam, long (Genesis 37:3; Exodus 29:5), and not to be divided or torn (Leviticus 21:10). In this manner, Jesus the eternal priest offers himself as a sacrifice for all humanity (Hebrews 4:14–5:10).

Jesus turns his attention to family and friends. In contrast to the other Gospels, Mary is mentioned before the death of Jesus; unlike Luke 23:49, she stands near the cross. (It is not clear if John is referring to three or four women in verse 25; three is usually understood.) In the midst of Jesus' severest agony, at the height of his hour, he is concerned for those close to him. Mary suggests or points attention to Jesus' true family, his followers, the true remnant of Israel, his brothers and sisters. Jesus' followers are then entrusted to the care and witness of the disciples—*Here is your mother*. Here, symbolically, is the actual working out of Jesus' priestly prayer (17:6-26).

Now comes the end of the hour. Jesus' kingly and priestly office has been proclaimed. His care for his family of followers is established. Everything is now ready for the ultimate sacrifice. Jesus requests a drink before his final fulfillment of Scripture. The drink is for quenching his thirst—a thirst that could only be fulfilled by doing God's will or reconciling the Father with humanity.

Jesus then states, *It is finished* (verse 30). He lowers his head and dies. In this final action, we find a wonderful symbol of Christ's work. His life is a prayer completed on our behalf, having completed the Father's will and lived a life of worship to the Father for all humanity. Similarly, when Jesus' followers pray bowing their heads, they are praying in the name of Christ and sacrificing their will for the will of the Father.

In the next section, Jesus is taken down from the cross. Like the lambs slaughtered for Passover, the sacrifice is now given final preparations. According to Jewish law, hanged criminals had to be removed from the tree (Deuteronomy 21:22-23). Romans tended to leave the criminals on the cross as a deterrent to others. But it was Passover, and the Jewish request was granted by Pilate. The two crucified with Jesus had their legs broken, perhaps because they were not yet dead (implied in verse 33).

The writer of the Gospel now affirms his witness. The sole purpose of his testimony is to help others understand and believe the person and mission of Jesus the Christ (20:30-31; 21:24). The writer also suggests his vital use of Scripture (that is, the Old Testament) in making sense out of what Christ taught and what Scripture anticipated. This Gospel concludes by quoting two texts relevant to Christ's sacrificial act: Exodus 12:46 and Zechariah 12:10.

The Burial (19:38-42)

Joseph of Arimathea and Nicodemus assist in the burial of Jesus. Joseph is identified as a *disciple.* According to the other Gospels, he seems to have been wealthy (Matthew 27:57), a member of the Sanhedrin (Mark 15:43; Luke 23:50), and he was sympathetic to Jesus (2:23–3:21).

These two Jewish officials, following Jewish burial customs, delicately prepare Christ's body with myrrh, aloes, and linen cloths. Jesus' body is prepared by these secret disciples, who are unaware that their work will be for nought. Jesus is placed in a garden tomb.

Everything is ready for something new to happen. Finally the tomb is closed. All this is in fulfillment of Jesus' hour; and it is only the day of preparation. This new day of preparation is followed by the old Passover, and then the wonderful new Passover. The old Passover was a time of fear, hiding, and danger for the disciples; the new Passover begins a time of jubilation, boldness, and courageous excitement.

§ § § § § § §

The Message of John 18–19

Jesus' hour is his time of suffering for humanity. He accomplishes two things.

From God's side, his hour is the time when the darkness of rebellion and sin in the creation come into direct confrontation with the will of God. He faces it all for us, as God came to humanity in order to bring us into right relationship. In this manner, God judges sin and rebellion, speaking a mighty "No!" to our sickness unto death.

From the human side, Jesus Christ, being without sin, takes our place and plows a path through our sin and rebellion leading a way back to the Father. Thus Jesus' arrest, trial, sufferings, crucifixion, and burial complete a life of worship to the Father that humanity was unable to live. Because God descended to us, living out that perfect life of fellowship and worship, Christ now reaches the bottom and is about to ascend with his (and therefore our) perfect humanity. He does this all for us. Now the preparations are complete.

§ § § § § § §

John 20

Introduction to This Chapter

The crucifixion cannot be understood apart from the Resurrection. Now that Christ has confronted sin and rebellion for humanity, now that he has suffered and died on our behalf, now that the case has been sent for deliberation, the disciples await the verdict. The news is overwhelming! He lives! This is God's eternal expression of grace following the judgment (the crucifixion) for humanity. This is the essence of the Gospel (Acts 2:23-24; Romans 1:4; 1 Corinthians 15:3-7), and must be seen in light of the ascension (Acts 1:6-11). Together these events are the good news, the new Passover.

Chapter 20 has three parts.

   I. Jesus Appears to Mary (20:1-18)

  II. Jesus Appears to the Disciples (20:19-29)

 III. The Signs of Jesus (20:30-31)

Jesus Appears to Mary (20:1-18)

What exactly happened on the first Easter morning? The four Gospel accounts vary somewhat with regard to the exact time of the morning, how many people went to the tomb, what was seen, what was spoken, and so forth (see Matthew 28; Mark 16:1-8; Luke 24).

Women first discover the empty tomb. In that day and age, men would have been more trustworthy for giving testimony of unusual events.

Things happen quickly, according to John's account. On the first day after Passover, one woman, Mary

Magdalene, comes to the tomb. This does not seem unusual because Jewish custom suggested mourning for the dead should peak on the third day. But it is significant that Mary comes when it is *dark*. For John's Gospel, the empty tomb has no real meaning or explanation for death.

Immediately Mary runs to Peter and *the other disciple* (verse 2). Both of these disciples were present in the courtyard when Jesus was interrogated by Annas and Caiaphas. Perhaps because of tomb robbers (who were a menace in the first century), or some other hostile group who disliked Jesus and his disciples, Mary assumes that the body has been stolen. She attributes the empty tomb to human activity. Her understanding is that Jesus is still dead, but she does not know where they have placed his body.

Peter and his companion run toward the tomb. John tells us that the other disciple runs faster than Peter, and when he reaches the tomb he does not enter. Peter arrives and boldly walks into the empty tomb, possibly a suggestion of Peter's future leadership of the church. He must stoop to enter, implying that the tomb or cave went down into the ground.

It must now be light—typical of Johannine symbolism—because they both see things in the empty tomb. What they see is significant. Unlike Lazarus, Jesus does not have to be unbound from the linen cloth. This he has done himself. The napkin or handkerchief-type towel that was placed on Jesus' head is found separate from the linen cloths.

The *beloved disciple* now enters the tomb. The wrappings and napkin in the tomb convince this other disciple that Jesus is risen. They have yet to understand what they see and witness. This understanding will come through Old Testament Scriptures. Then we are told the disciples return home or return to their lodgings.

Perhaps they need time to digest what they have seen and sensed.

Now Mary returns to the scene. She is weeping outside the tomb. Stoping to look in, she sees something different from what the disciples saw. Two angels are present, apparently to help her understand what has happened. The angels are dressed in white, indicating that they are sent from God (Ezekiel 9:2; Daniel 10:5). One sits at the head and one sits at the foot of where Jesus has lain.

The angels question Mary. Their question eventually leads her to confront Jesus, much like the work of Jesus' disciples will lead humanity to confront Jesus. They ask her why she is so sad. She explains simply that Jesus, the *Lord*, is gone; he is not here. In making her statement, she is *turned round*, and unknowingly confronts Jesus, who has been transformed. In this scene, she represents all humanity. As we seek answers to the great questions of life, we are automatically turned to face Jesus the Christ—often unknowingly.

Then Jesus questions her: *Why are you weeping? Whom are you looking for?* His questions to Mary suggest that he has the answers—in fact, his questions suggest that he is the answer. Mary wants the answers to this puzzle she faces, the puzzle of life. She thinks he is the gardener, recalling the Old Testament story of God maintaining the Garden of Eden. Jesus questions Mary in the same manner that God questioned Adam and Eve: *Where are you?* (Genesis 3:9). Mary offers to take the body back, perhaps a statement meant to discount any suggestion that the body was stolen. Jesus then calls her by name. She immediately recognizes Jesus' personal address to her and the one who addresses her. Hearing Jesus address her, she turns and calls him *teacher*, a strong term of deep appreciation best translated *my dear teacher*.

Jesus tells Mary not to touch him. Their previous friendship must now change. No longer can they touch him as they did when he was with them before. Now they have a new relationship that will be characterized by Jesus ascending to the Father on their behalf. So Mary cannot hold onto Jesus. He must go. Then Mary immediately goes and bears witness to the Christ.

Jesus Appears to the Disciples (20:19-29)

Now the narrative moves to the evening of the Resurrection day. The disciples have had all day to talk about what happened in the garden to Mary, Peter, and the beloved disciple. Perhaps the Emmaus road incident had happened during the day (Luke 24:13-35). It is *evening* (verse 19), just before sunset. The night is about to come. The disciples are frightened of what is out there—the hostile world. But their strength to face the hostile world is in Jesus, their resurrected Lord.

Jesus comes and stands among them, saying *Peace be with you.* His very presence with them is peace. And when he ascends to the Father, he will always be in their midst through the counselor, the Spirit of Truth, who will keep them in the peace he has established between the Father and them (14:27).

Jesus witnesses to them concerning what he has done. He shows them the wounds of his confrontation with sin and rebellion. The disciples are glad that evil no longer has any power to separate them from God. The happy disciples again receive the peace from the risen Christ. His second statement of peace refers back to the wounds Jesus has just shown them. His life and death will bring them peace because they are now reconciled to the Father. And his peace refers ahead to the task they are given. As the Father sent Christ to reconcile God with humanity, God now sends his disciples out as witnesses of his completed work.

But Jesus does not leave them to their own resources. He gives them the promised Holy Spirit. They are not meant to become examples, or ends in themselves, as

144

witnesses to Christ. Their task is not to establish their own following. They are meant to point others to Christ. The disciples are told that their witness will lead to some being forgiven and some retaining their sins. The authority for such forgiveness is not in the disciples, but only in their true witness of pointing others to Christ. In their witness they will see results all around them.

Thomas is a perfect example of unbelief. John tells us that Thomas was absent when Jesus visited with the disciples. Those disciples who were with him give their testimony, but Thomas makes his statement that unless he gets much more evidence, he will not believe. Like Mary in the garden, Thomas does not recognize Jesus through the disciples' testimony. Two future problems are evident here. The disciples' testimony will often fall on deaf ears. How could Thomas have doubted his friends' testimony about the person whom they all had followed? Yet Thomas doubts. He has chosen not to respond to the testimony of the disciples.

The story of Thomas concludes with Jesus returning to the disciples. Events identical with Jesus' previous visit happen, affirming the disciples' testimony: The doors are closed, and Jesus comes into their midst and gives them his peace. Jesus now repeats Thomas's earlier statements, reversing the skepticism. Previously Jesus had told Mary not to touch him. Why the difference?

Thomas is being encouraged to get on with his apostolic witness. Mary immediately goes to bear witness to the disciples, and the disciples accept the witness of the empty tomb. Thomas remains distant, demanding more substance to the disciples' testimony. This incident seems to suggest that Jesus' disciples must not make certain demands before they bear witness to Christ's work of reconciliation.

Thomas immediately responds to Jesus' presence. Jesus then speaks about those who believe and yet do not see. Thomas personifies those who wish to place conditions for belief on the risen Christ. But the conditions persons wish to place on the Christ are human distractions to belief, and therefore are distractions for bearing witness to Christ. Conditions for belief in Christ are determined by Christ alone, and not humanity (thus Jesus' questioning of Mary).

The Signs of Jesus (20:30-31)

Finally in this section we find what appears to be a conclusion to the Gospel. *Signs* would seem to refer to Jesus' activities after his resurrection. It must be remembered that this is the last Gospel written. During the later years of the first century, gnosticism (see the glossary) began to influence Christianity. This influence tended to "spiritualize" the Resurrection. John seems to be carefully pointing out that the resurrection of Jesus was factual. It happened in time and space. It is substantiated by the many signs that John records here: the empty tomb, the experience of the two disciples and Mary, Jesus' visits with the disciples, and so forth. The actual physical Resurrection is re-emphasized in the incident with Thomas. And there are many other signs that Jesus did. There were just too many to record.

Then the Gospel of John states its only purpose. It was written for one reason: that those who read may come to believe in the real identity and mission of Jesus of Nazareth. This Jesus was the Christ, the Messiah, the Son of God who came to give eternal life (1 John 5:13).

§ § § § § § §

The Message of John 20

The Resurrection is the first half of God's almighty and eternal "Yes!" to humanity; the resurrection and ascension are the full "Yes!" of God to humanity. And this almighty "Yes!" brings us back to where the Gospel began: *In the beginning was the Word, and the Word was with God, and the Word was God* (1:1).

With the Resurrection and the ascension, *the Word* comes full circle back to where it all began. Christ descended for humanity. Now Christ ascends for humanity. Thus the Resurrection must be seen in the light of the ascension and in the light of the crucifixion.

In the crucifixion, God says, "Absolutely not!" to human rebellion and sin. But the resounding "Yes!" is spoken much louder, much more clearly, and with eternal finality. Christ's resurrection begins the new age of eternal life and peace through Holy Spirit.

Christ now goes to the Father. During his absence, his followers have a mission. They are to work bearing witness to him. All humanity is called to believe in him and bear witness to his work of reconciliation, now complete. This "Yes!" to humanity shouted in the Resurrection and completed in the ascension is the heart of the Christian good news.

§ § § § § § §

John 21

Introduction to This Chapter

This final chapter is sometimes called the epilogue of
John's Gospel. It has two parts.
I. Jesus with the Disciples Beside the Sea (21:1-14)
II. The Command to Follow Jesus (21:15-25)
Some have argued that this chapter is a later editorial
addition to the Gospel, suggested by an apparent ending
to the book at the conclusion of the previous chapter.
Perhaps this account was based upon an incident John
once told his disciples, and the disciples added it to the
Gospel after John's death. But there is no real evidence to
suggest that this section (along with John 8:1-11) is
anything other than a legitimate account of an experience
the disciples remembered. The fact that a similar account
occurs prior to the Resurrection in the other Gospels may
have helped reinforce the importance of this recollection
(Matthew 8:24-27; Mark 4:35-41; Luke 5:1-10).

This account is the third post-Resurrection appearance.
In this particular appearance, the disciples are given a
commission to start working. In this manner, the Gospel
of John explains to us how Christ will not leave his
church desolate (14:18), but will provide for all its needs
as the body of Christ.

Jesus with the Disciples by the Sea (21:1-14)

In the first few verses, the stage is set for what is about
to happen. The scene is introduced by the words,

Afterward (NIV; NRSV, *After these things*). Following the "ending" in the last chapter, this section is joined to what has already been stated. There is no suggestion of the time that has passed since the previous events. But it is clearly stated that Jesus appears again at this particular place, the *Sea of Tiberias*. The Sea of Tiberias is called the *Sea of Galilee* earlier (6:1) in this Gospel. This was the sea on which Jesus walked (6:16-21). On that occasion, Jesus *withdrew again to the mountain* because some wanted to make him king (6:15).

Five disciples are together, suggesting some form of fellowship. This is further suggested when they enter the boat together, the boat being a symbol of the church in the early years of Christianity. On the previous occasion when they were together on the lake, their purpose was to cross the water, or more precisely, pass through life. But now they have a more exact mission: Now they are going fishing (verse 3). Fish also carried some importance in the early church. Peter takes the initiative and makes the statement. This intention states their new calling, spoken when they became disciples (Luke 5:10). They get into the boat, and during the night, or in the dark, they catch nothing. Launching out on their own, they have no success in the darkness. In a previous situation, they had the same problem until Jesus gave the word (see Luke 5:5). It is only the dawning of the light that will change the situation.

The "dawning" is the theme of the next section. Just as day is breaking, Jesus appears on the beach (verse 4). He questions them, calling them *children* as he did before when he told them about his going away (13:33). It is significant that throughout the Gospel accounts, the disciples never catch a fish without Jesus' help. The disciples' answer to Jesus is a simple No.

Jesus gives them orders to fish off the *right side* of the boat. Casting their net on the right side, they are unable to haul in the fish. Immediately Jesus is recognized, this time by the beloved disciple and not Peter (verse 7). This recognition gives the beloved disciple leadership and importance. But it is Peter who responds with the most energy. He immediately puts on his *clothes,* a reference to his robe or priestly tunic. Similar to Jesus' clothes at the cross (19:23-24), Peter's clothes signify his leadership in the church. Leaving the boat in an almost missionary fashion, he springs into the dark, rebellious sea. The other disciples are stewards of the catch. They return to the shore where Jesus is, bringing *the net full of fish.* The other four disciples' responsibility is to take care of the church's needs (or the craft's needs).

In the next scene, the disciples are on the shore with Jesus. As noted in chapter 6, when Jesus entered the boat they immediately reached their destination. Jesus is their destination (10:1; 14:6). What does this mean? It means that Jesus provides all their needs. Because he is the bread of life, he provides breakfast food for the disciples who have arrived on the new shore in the dawning light.

What the disciples see on the shore is important. They see a charcoal fire (verse 9). But the fire Jesus prepares is not for keeping warm in the cold night air. The purpose of Jesus' fire is to prepare the fish and warm the bread. The *bread of life* (6:35) is now preparing the very fish he has directed them to catch.

Peter goes aboard the boat that symbolizes the church. He hauls the fish to the shore. The Gospel suggests no need for superhuman strength in retrieving the fish from the net—even the net remains untorn. The emphasis is not on the disciples who catch the fish, though they do the work; the catching of the fish is accomplished by obeying the directives of Jesus. The text reads that there are about 153 large fish. This seems to exact for an "about" figure, and seems to imply that every fish is important (10:14-15).

Jesus then invites them to have breakfast. The disciples have fasted during the night while laboring on the treacherous sea. The meaning here is similar to the teachings of John the Baptist (3:29), suggesting that the disciples must fast and labor when the bridegroom is away with the Father. But the bridegroom will remain close to his bride (the church) and constantly supply food that will one day break the fast forever, and become a full banquet (when he returns). Thus Jesus actually gives the disciples their sustenance, represented by the bread (his body) and the fish (their work) he has supplied (verse 13).

This is the third time Jesus has appeared to the disciples. In the Jewish tradition, three is a number of perfection, wholeness, and completeness. After Jesus' third appearance to the disciples, his post-Resurrection revelations will be complete. The disciples do not easily recognize Jesus on this third visitation. Perhaps, in these unusual circumstances, Jesus seems out of place. Jesus has now come to them on their own terms, in the place where they live, speaking to them through his unexpected presence. This, plus his new resurrected and transformed state, may have momentarily confused the disciples.

The Command to Follow Jesus (21:15-25)

In this final section of the Gospel, Peter receives his direct commission. After breakfast, Jesus questions the disciples. Although his questions are directed to Peter, this disciple is the spokesperson of the others and therefore all are questioned. Jesus initially probes Peter's love for him: *Do you love me more than these?* In verses 16-17 Jesus' question is simply, *Do you love me?* Three times Peter is asked the question and three times he will respond and three times he will be told what to do. The "threeness" of the answer suggests completeness and wholeness, as noted above. These are tremendous questions in the midst of a powerful scene—the scene of everyday life. The three questions also seem to counter Peter's threefold denial before the crucifixion.

Peter is really being asked by Jesus if he properly and fully understands who Jesus is, and who Peter is in relation to Jesus. Peter has claimed that he would die for Jesus (13:36-38). Yet, he fell asleep in the garden when Jesus prayed (Mark 14:32-42); he denied Jesus three times (18:17, 25-27); and he was in hiding with the rest of the disciples after Jesus died, and perhaps even after he witnessed the empty tomb (20:19).

Peter is expected to respond. He says three times, *You know that I love you.* Each time Peter seems to be a little more put out, until the last time when he says that Jesus knows, because he knows everything. Each question seems to move Peter into a deeper realization of what Jesus is asking and what Peter is telling Jesus. Each question demands Peter to speak out and answer Jesus' address to him. Each time Peter and the other disciples—and the reader—hear Peter's response. And the response itself focuses everything on Jesus to the extent that Peter becomes a small "i": *You know that i love you!*

But Peter is not allowed to just talk. After each reply of Peter, Jesus tells him exactly what to do: Feed and tend my lambs and sheep. The directive Jesus gives recalls his saying recorded throughout chapter 10, where he explains himself as the shepherd of the sheep. Because they are his sheep who accept his reconciling work, the disciples are instructed to care for them. They are meant to become the shepherds of the sheep. This is clear throughout the dialogue. Their task is to love the Christ *more than these* by confessing and bearing witness to his lordship, and therefore directing the sheep to trust and follow the shepherd.

After clarifying his own identity and the disciples' true identity, he now directs them to get on with it by getting to work. *Feed my sheep* is stated three times, implying wholeness and completeness. The terms *sheep* (converts) and *lamb* and *shepherd* (Christ) are prominent terms in important Old Testament books (Isaiah, Jeremiah, Ezekiel, and Zechariah), and in the book of Revelation (see especially Revelation 6:16 and 17:14).

Then, using the double *amen,* Jesus predicts Peter's death (verses 18-19). Jesus uses contrasts here between putting on one's belt and having it put on, going somewhere and being taken, going where one wishes and where one does not wish. These contrasts suggest following the Father's will wherever it may lead. The *outstretched hands* may be a reference to the manner in which Peter died. A third-century church leader wrote of Peter being bound with a belt and crucified. These verses also suggest that the Gospel was written after Peter's death.

Then Jesus concludes this part of the dialogue with *Follow me,* a statement probably directed to all the disciples.

They are now apparently walking along the shore. Peter turns and sees the *disciple whom Jesus loved* and asks Jesus about his role (verse 21). Jesus makes it clear that not only does he have a different calling, but his calling should not in any way disturb or affect Peter's work and calling. Jesus goes even further. He explains that if it is his will that the other disciple should live long, even until the time when Jesus returns, what difference can this make to Peter's responsibilities before the Father?

For John's audience, these verses may have offered two other explanations. First of all, they distinguish the responsibilities of the beloved disciple and Peter. They have different callings, and the followers of John may have needed to know this. Second, it is possible that this chapter was added after John's death and initial writing of the Gospel. These verses would have explained to the readers of this Gospel, who were probably taught by

John, that his death should not deafen the ears to the Gospel.

The author then puts his final statement on the Gospel. If this chapter was added later, this verse may very well be a summary statement of what John taught his parishioners. Furthermore, it is a restatement of John's particular role or calling implied by Jesus. John was eventually called to abide. Peter was called to bear witness in a spoken and active form—a pastoral form—that Jesus was the Christ. Thus they had different callings, different places to go, and different work to do. And so with all Jesus' disciples.

This chapter concludes with what appears to be another ending of John (verse 25). This statement may suggest one of two things: (1) that early believers were straining to get more information about Jesus the Christ. Here they are assured that there is much more than happened, but this information is sufficient to achieve the intended purpose—bearing witness to Jesus as the Christ. (2) The writer and editors shaped the information along Jewish festival lines, identifying signs that showed Jesus fulfilling Jewish messianic expectations.

§ § § § § § §

The Message of John 21

Here we find the full commission of Jesus' disciples. They are called to bear witness to him at all times and in all places. Needs will be supplied—both spiritual and physical—based on particular calling. In order to bear witness, they must come to know fully who he is and who they are in relation to him. This happens continually and constantly, before, during, and after Jesus speaks the words, *Follow me!*

§ § § § § § §

Glossary of Terms

Aramaic: A language closely related to Hebrew, originating in northern Syria among the ancestors of Abraham. Jesus probably spoke a "western" dialect of Aramaic.

Babylonian Captivity (the Exile): In the sixth century B.C., Nebuchadnezzar conquered Judah and deported its leadership to Babylon. They did not return for at least forty years.

Circumcision: Many Eastern nations have practiced this cultic act of removing the foreskin from the penis. The reason for Israel's practice has been lost, but some references suggest it was a sign for keeping the covenant and to ward off evil.

Dead Sea Scrolls: These are Scriptures found in caves at the northwest end of the Dead Sea between 1947 and 1960. They include many Old Testament books and other writings and date from the late 200s B.C. to A.D. 70.

Essene: This Jewish sect was active from the Maccabean period (160s B.C.) to the Roman destruction of Jerusalem (A.D. 70). This may be the group that authored the Dead Sea Scrolls and lived at Qumran. It has been suggested—although there is no evidence—that John the Baptist and possibly Jesus were associated with this group.

Father: This is the name Jesus used for God. *Abba* is the Aramaic term that is preserved in our Greek New Testament and is better translated *Daddy*. Jesus taught his disciples to address God with this term, even though Jews did not even say the name of God because this implied power over the one addressed.

Feast of Dedication: Also called *Hanukkah*, this feast celebrates the purification of the Temple by the Maccabees in the 160s B.C. It celebrates Jewish freedom to worship their God.

Feast of Tabernacles: Also called *Ingathering* or *Booths*, this is a major pilgrimage festival for visiting Jerusalem. The eight-day event celebrates the harvest and God's protection of Israel during the wilderness wanderings.

Fish: In the Old Testament, the fish is associated with the freshness of water. The death of fish can contaminate water and once caused a death plague (Exodus 7:21) and a drought (Isaiah 50:2). In the early church, the fish became a sign of Christ. The Greek word for fish, *ichthys,* was understood to mean *Jesus Christ, God's son, savior.*

Genre: A type of literature. The Christian Gospels are a particular genre that attempts to tell readers who Jesus of Nazareth really was and what he accomplished.

Gnosticism: This term refers to many groups active during the first centuries of Christianity. Although diverse in beliefs, they generally offered freedom from material pollution through a special saving *knowledge* (Greek term, *gnosis*). This knowledge offered a special relationship with the god of the universe. A type of gnosticism seems to have been active in Ephesus, where John's Gospel was probably written.

Gospel: The Greek word *evangelion* means *good news* and translates as *gospel.* The four New Testament Gospels are carefully written (Luke 1:1-4), and each has a particular purpose (John 20:30-31; 21:24-25).

Greek language: The New Testament was written in a dialect of Greek called *Koine,* or Hellenistic Greek. *Koine* means *common,* and was brought to Palestine by Alexander the Great (died 323 B.C.). It remained a universal language until the 500s A.D. Jesus may have been bilingual, speaking both Aramaic and Koine Greek.

Hellenism: This term refers to the spread of Greek culture throughout the lands Alexander the Great conquered, including Palestine.

High Priest: This was the head official who performed Temple rituals, especially sacrifices. Traditionally, priests were Levites who received no land (Deuteronomy 10:8-9). During Jesus' time, the high priest was also the head of local government, the collector of taxes, and the one who dealt with ruling powers.

I Am: This is the Old Testament name for God given to Moses (Exodus 3:14) and probably is the basis for the Hebrew name for God, *Yahweh*. The phrase indicates the "mystery" of God (Genesis 32:22-32), and when used by Jesus suggests equality with God.

Levites: Members of the family of Levi, one of the sons of Jacob. The members of this family had a right to the priesthood (Deuteronomy 10:8-9).

Messiah: This term comes from a Hebrew word that means *anointed one* and refers to being anointed by God. The Greek translation is *Christos*, or *Christ*.

New Year Festival: Also known as *Rosh Hashanah*, meaning *the beginning of the year*. Celebrated in the fall, it was a time of sacrifices and trumpet blasts.

Passover: This is the greatest Jewish festival, recalling God's deliverance of Israel from Egypt. A Passover sacrifice was part of the ritual in celebration of how God protected the people.

Pentecost: Combined in the early Old Testament with the feast of Weeks, it came to be known in Jesus' time as God's "historical relationship" with Israel. After the Temple was destroyed in A.D. 70, it became a celebration of God's having given the Torah or law. For early Christians, it was the coming of the Holy Spirit (Acts 2:1-42).

Pharisees: A group of Jews who were rigorous in the keeping of the law. Probably only a small part of this religiously devout group clashed with Jesus.

Prologue: This refers to an introduction before the main events. In John's Gospel, the prologue (1:1-18) introduces the various recollections of Jesus' life.

Sacrifice: Some form of sacrifice is a basic means of communicating with a deity in all religions. For Israel, this was their primary form of worshiping God.

Samaria: This was the region of northern Israel settled by Joseph. Assyria conquered the Northern Kingdom in 722 B.C., bringing in colonists and deporting Israelites.

Sanhedrin: In the New Testament, the term refers to a council of leaders and elders who oversaw Israel and its traditions.

Shechem: An early Jewish shrine, this city became the religious center of the Samaritans (after 350 B.C.; see John 4).

Sheep: The most commonly mentioned animal in the Bible. The New Testament uses sheep to designate persons. John's Gospel portrays Jesus as the Shepherd who gives his life for the sheep. Jesus is also portrayed as a sheep led to the slaughter (Acts 8:32; Isaiah 53:7).

Sheep Gate: Once a gate on Jerusalem's north city wall near the Temple (Nehemiah 3:1). Sheep for sacrifice were probably brought into the Temple courtyard through this gate.

Sign: An indication of God's presence or God's will. In the New Testament, signs are usually miracles. John's Gospel records seven signs that Jesus did: changing water into wine (2:1-11); healing the official's son (4:46-54); healing the paralytic (5:1-15); multiplying the loaves (6:1-15); walking on the sea (6:16-21); curing a blind man (9:1-4); and raising Lazarus from the dead (11:1-44).

Son of God: This refers to a special relationship between God and either a biblical person or the nation Israel. Jesus, the pre-existent son, is the person who has the special relationship with the Father.

Son of man: Jesus' phrase in reference to himself. It is a phrase asserting Jesus' full humanity, and it has definite Old Testament overtones (see Psalm 8:4; Daniel 7:9-14).

Spirit (Holy Spirit): God's Spirit is sent by the Father and the Son, and represents God's presence and activity.

Temple: The term refers to the center of Jewish religious life. It was understood as the place where God dwells on earth. The Temple was a center for Jesus' activities, according to John's Gospel.

Truly, truly: According to John's Gospel, this is an expression frequently used by Jesus. It literally means, *amen, amen,* or *absolutely, certainly,* or *so be it.* Jesus uses it in a unique way, offsetting his teachings.

Guide to Pronunciation

Abba: AH-buh
Aenon: EYE-non
Annas: ANN-us
Bethesda: Beh-THEHZ-dah
Bethsaida: Beth-SAY-ih-dah
Bethzatha: Beth-ZAH-thah
Caiaphas: KAY-ih-fuss
Cana: KAY-nah
Capernaum: Kah-PER-nay-um
Cephas: SEE-fuss
Clopas: KLOH-pas
Denarii: Deh-NAIR-ee
Ephesus: EH-feh-suss
Ephraim: Ee-frah-EEM
Hanukkah: HAH-nah-kuh
Judea: Joo-DEE-ah
Lystra: LISS-trah
Maccabees: MACK-ah-beez
Magdalene: MAG-dah-lehn
Malchus: MAHL-kuss
Nathanael: Nah-THAN-yell
Pharisees: FAIR-eh-seez
Salim: SAY-lehm
Samaria: Sah-MARE-ee-ah
Sanhedrin: San-HEE-drin
Shechem: SHEH-kem
Siloam: Sih-LOH-am
Sychar: SIGH-kar

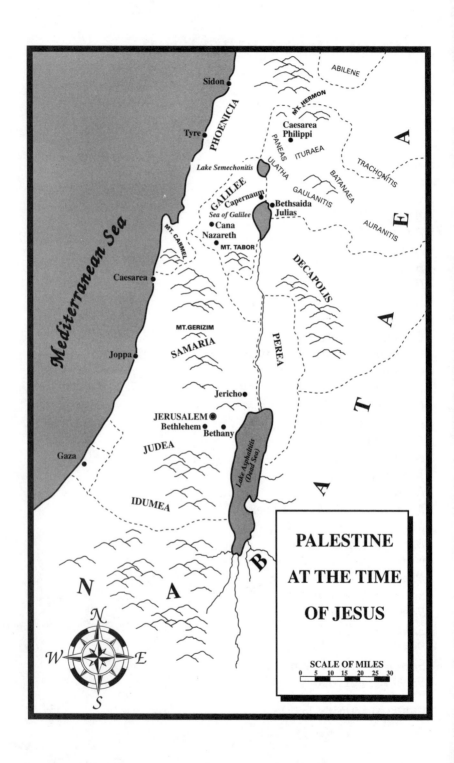

Sidon

PHOENICIA

Tyre

MT. HERMON

ABILENE

Caesarea
Philippi

PANEAS

ITURAEA

TRACHONITIS

Lake Semechonitis

ULATHA

BATANAEA

GALILEE

Capernaum

GAULANITIS

AURANITIS

Mediterranean Sea

Sea of Galilee

Bethsaida
Julias

Cana

Nazareth

MT. TABOR

MT. CARMEL

DECAPOLIS

Caesarea

MT.GERIZIM

SAMARIA

PEREA

Joppa

Jericho

JERUSALEM
Bethlehem

Bethany

Gaza

JUDEA

Lake Asphaltitis
(Dead Sea)

IDUMEA

NABATA

N

A

B

PALESTINE

AT THE TIME

OF JESUS

SCALE OF MILES

0   5   10 15 20 25 30

N

W   E

S